# GUIDE TO WINTER CLIMBS

# BEN NEVIS

# and GLENCOE

## by IAN CLOUGH

REVISED BY **HAMISH MacINNES**

Illustrated by R. B. Evans

**cp**

First Edition March 1969
Reprinted April 1969, April 1970
Second (Revised) Edition March 1971
Reprinted December 1976
**Reprinted 1978**

902363 03 4

Cover: Ian Clough on first ascent of Sabre Tooth, Glencoe
(Photo. H. MacInnes)

Published by Cicerone Press
Harmony Hall, Milnthorpe, Cumbria LA7 7QE, England

# CONTENTS

# FOREWORD

I have always felt that the best memorial to a man is what he leaves to society. This guide is an example of Ian Clough's thoroughness and his dedication to mountaineering. His other less obvious contribution was his devotion to his climbing clients over the years and the knowledge which he passed on to them.

It would be imprudent of me to do any major alteration to this guide even if I wanted to. However, several routes have been added—for I know Ian wanted this—and with the passing of time various addresses etc. have changed. Route lengths have also been revised in some cases.

I trust that the user of this guide will derive as much pleasure in doing these climbs as Ian and I did.

Hamish MacInnes

Glencoe, 1970

# INTRODUCTION

Ben Nevis and the peaks of Glencoe give some of the finest winter mountaineering in Britain. The mountains are bigger than those of England and Wales and can generally be relied upon to retain a good covering of permanent snow from December until April or May. The original pioneers tended to regard Scottish snow climbing as good training for greater mountaineering but winter climbing as practised in Scotland today has developed into a very specialised sub-sport and many now consider that the Alps can provide useful training for Scottish ice!

Many of the longer routes are more alpine than British in length and character. But Scottish winter mountaineering can be even more serious than climbing in the Alps. The weather is often precarious and blizzards of arctic ferocity can strike with startling suddenness, transforming a pleasant excursion into a battle for existence. Too many people underestimate the Scottish mountains, too many have died Even expert parties, climbing in good weather, have had their epics due to unexpected conditions of heavy icing high on the route. There are many embarrassing stories of famous men, Himalayan veterans too, getting themselves into trouble on Ben Nevis. One such was so impressed that he remarked that if a man could climb safely on the Ben in winter then he could climb safely anywhere in the world. There may have been an element of rueful cynicism behind this remark for the unfortunate gentleman had just broken his leg.

A combination of short daylight hours and the danger of a break in the weather gives Scottish winter climbing an alpine-like urgency. Speed is the critical factor and because of this there is no need for an artificial code of rules such as is applied to British rock climbing. The ethics of the Alps have been adopted; pegs and screws may be used at will but one must bear in mind that the use of such aids mean delay and a bivouac could result in serious consequences. Speed is as vital as in the Alps and, although times can vary enormously according to the conditions encountered, a fast time is the criterion of ability. Conversely, a slow time is generally a sign of incompetence.

## Conditions of Snow and Ice

To the winter mountaineer, a thorough knowledge of snow structures is vital. Not only does this knowledge help him to estimate avalanche risk but also enables him to select the routes most likely to be in condition. The following summary may be helpful but climbers preparing for a Scottish winter holiday would be well advised to read and study **The Avalanche Enigma** by Colin Frazer, which gives easy reading and contains much useful information relevant to snow and ice mountaineering.

The different types of snow and ice commonly met in Britain can be very simply categorised:-

1. Fresh fallen snow.  2. Settled snow.  3. Firn snow.
4. White Ice.  5. Green Ice.

There are many different varieties of snow and ice in each of these general categories. Verglas is caused by raindrops falling on frozen ground and usually forms a very thin transparent veneer although it can become quite thick. Black Ice is caused by the freezing of drainage water. Both these ice conditions are exceptionally tough and make climbing very difficult as natural holds are covered and yet the skin of the ice is generally too thin to allow steps to be cut.

"Ideal conditions" consist of hard-packed Firn Snow or White Ice (both commonly referred to as névé). This is the best material for the cutting of sound steps and is perfect for cramponing. Unfortunately these conditions do not occur all that frequently even in Scotland and early climbers were often very frustrated. When lacking firn snow in the gullies, great sport can be had on ridges, buttresses and faces — battling with powder snow, verglassed rocks and frozen vegetation. When spells of hard frost prevent the snows of the upper corries from consolidating, low-level watercourses can provide interesting high standard climbing on brittle ice. Some of the climbs included in this selection are scarcely worthy of attention if conditions are good at higher levels; they have been chosen deliberately as interesting alternatives to floundering through deep powder snow.

## Avalanches

Avalanches occur far more frequently in Scotland than most people realise and the number of avalanche accidents is on the increase. "Spindrift" or powder snow avalanches are common but rarely assume serious proportions. It is possible for them to be large enough to sweep a leader from his steps but normally they are uncomfortable rather than dangerous. The worst type of avalanche on the West Coast is of the wet snow variety. Often these are fairly predictable; caused by cornices collapsing in heavy thaw conditions. However, avalanche conditions may develop much more subtly. Rain or meltwater, percolating down through a soft layer of snow and then running over the surface of a tougher underlying layer can break most of the anchorage between the two. Often the upper layer, although appearing to be quite safe, may only be supported by friction at its edges and can break away without warning. There are several other processes which lead to dangerously unstable snow conditions: Ground Hoar (hard, ball-bearing-like granules) may develop between layers of snow; Windslab is notoriously dangerous but fortunately it is less common on the West Coast than in the Cairngorms; Wet-Slab is a similar condition, prevalent during or just after a snow fall. As a rough guide the following are sensible precautions to avoid the risk of avalanche:

1. Do not attempt to climb during, or until at least 24 hours after, a heavy snow fall.

2. Avoid gullies during periods of thaw, especially if they are known to carry large cornices. The ridges and buttresses will usually provide safe alternatives.

3. Probing the slope with the ice axe shaft can often reveal some-

thing of the composition of the snow layers and give an indication of potential avalanche danger. Easy penetration of the lower snow may indicate a loosely anchored slope. If, on waggling the axe, the snow makes a creaking sound, then in all probability it is of slab formation. If you have doubts about the condition of a slope (sometimes the ice axe shaft will not be long enough to give a proper indication of the state of the lower layers) then it would be wise to cut a deep section for further inspection or to retreat carefully.

Apart from the risk of avalanches, winter mountaineers are susceptible to other objective dangers normally only associated with the Alps. Strong sunlight particularly can bring danger in the form of falling stones and chunks of ice. But knowledge of snow structure, shrewd judgement and, above all, experience, reduce all these risks to an acceptable level.

## Equipment, Clothing and Safety Precautions

It is assumed that nobody would consider attempting winter climbs without an ice-axe and crampons (or boots nailed with Tricounis) and the knowledge of how to use them properly. A hammer and a selection of pegs (and screws for the more difficult climbs) should also be regarded as standard equipment. A metal ice axe belay is possibly adequate for the easy climbs where a falling leader can be expected to arrest himself to some extent, but wherever possible a rock belay should be sought. It is often difficult and time consuming to find natural belays and usually easier to insert a peg. On exceptionally steep ice it is common practice to use a screw or peg to maintain balance whilst cutting steps and they are also used as running belays.

Adequate clothing of a suitable kind is a necessity. This includes woollen gloves, overmitts and balaclava; spare mitts or gloves are useful. A duvet jacket or extra sweater and emergency rations should be carried against the possibility of weather deterioration or forced bivouac and a large polythene bag or bivouac sac could prove a life-saver. Although every precaution should be taken to avoid their use becoming necessary, it is sensible to carry a headtorch and spare batteries to enable a climb to be finished in darkness. Other normal safety equipment should be carried; whistle or flares for emergency and a map and compass. **It is essential to have a sound knowledge of navigation.**

'White-out' conditions (when visibility is so poor that snow and sky merge into one) are common and it is often a wise precaution to keep the rope on during the descent. In this way a party can 'feel' their way along the cliff-top, one man cautiously edging along near the cornices whilst belayed by the rest of his party. It should be unnecessary to emphasise the dangers of cornices.

There are more accidents in descent than from any other cause. Be sure you have identified the correct gully for descent and always proceed with extreme caution. If in doubt, it is preferable to take the long way round, go down by the way you came or even, as a last resort, remain where you are until visibility improves. But remember, if caught in a blizzard, that storms can last for several days.

Never, never glissade unless you can see all the way down the slope (and even then crags may be hidden) and you are positive that there is no ice about. Before you set out on your climb study the notes on descents and accident procedure given in the introduction to each area or mountain and make sure that your proposed route is known to others.

# NOTES ON THE USE OF THE GUIDE

**Gradings:** I have not used the conventional grading system as applied to rock climbs but have adopted the system used for grading winter routes in the Cairngorms and on Creag Meaghaidh. Winter routes should not be compared with rock climbs; a top standard rock leader is still a comparative novice on snow and ice until he has served his apprenticeship. Also, the difficulty of winter routes can vary drastically according to conditions. It is neither possible nor desirable to categorise them anything like so accurately as rock climbs. **The grades used here are for average conditions and the standard of the climb may vary considerably either way.** Factors taken into consideration in addition to technical difficulty are:- length, route-finding problems, concentration of difficulty and seriousness (i.e. lack of good protection and belays). Even Grade III routes may contain a pitch of the highest technical standard. The grades have been allocated in consultation with experienced climbers from the Cairngorms and thus the two systems should be comparable. The system is outlined below:—

**Grade I:** Generally straight-forward, uniform but sometimes steep slopes of snow or ice or exceptionally easy ridges. Even these climbs may involve serious cornice problems.

**Grade II:** Fairly difficult climbs involving short pitches and/or route-finding problems.

**Grade III:** Serious routes which should not be undertaken except by experienced parties.

**Grade IV:** Exacting climbs of sustained severity or climbs of the highest standard which are too short or lack the seriousness to merit Grade V.

**Grade V:** Formidable undertakings, often only feasible in exceptionally favourable conditions. The only rock equivalent would be the old 'Exceptionally' grade. **Except for passing mention, routes in this category are not described or recommended; parties competent to attempt them will do so on their own responsibility and without need of guidance.**

**Times.** As a further aid to estimating the difficulty of a climb, a time (based on a competent Scottish pair, leading-through, in average conditions) has been given after each grading. This is only a very rough guide and times can vary drastically with changed conditions. Many English parties will probably find that they take longer than these suggested times and should make allowances accordingly.

**Recommendations.** All the routes included in this selection are well worthwhile but some are much better than others. A star system of quality recommendation has been adopted as follows: * Good, ** Very good, *** Excellent. (see index).

**Rope Lengths.** 120 ft. of rope between two climbers is usually adequate except on some of the more serious routes where 150 ft. is preferable. The use of a double rope is recommended for the increased protection it can afford and for facilitating retreat by abseil.

**Lengths of Climbs.** The figure given is often only roughly estimated. Wherever possible, lengths are judged in terms of climbing distance (i.e. rope lengths) rather than by vertical height.

**Left and Right Directions.** The terms **left** and **right** apply to a climber facing inwards (towards the cliff or upstream) unless specifically stated otherwise. Left and right are abbreviated in the text to l. and r.

**First Ascents.** The parties here credited with ascents are generally those who made the first winter ascent.

**Season.** The season can extend from November through until May and it is impossible to forecast what month might bring the best conditions. One year I experienced the best conditions of the whole season in mid December whereas the conditions in 1968 only became really good in late April. However, it can generally be assumed that until late January there will be no great build-up of snow and that climbs, particularly gullies, may be more difficult due to the existence of pitches which would normally be obliterated later on. The gradings and times are given for average conditions and if you are climbing early in the season this should be borne in mind.

**Maps and other Guidebooks.** The One-inch O.S. Tourist Sheet **Lorn and Lochaber** includes both areas and is the recommended map. Bartholomew's Half-inch Maps (Sheets 51, 50, 48 and 47) are very useful for those wishing to identify surrounding mountains but are not detailed enough for accurate navigation.

This guidebook only gives a limited selection of the winter routes available on Ben Nevis and in Glencoe. A definitive series of climbers' guidebooks is published by The Scottish Moutaineering Trust, giving details of all winter and summer climbs and general information regarding the mountains in all areas of Scotland. A list of these publications, including forthcoming volumes, is given below:—

Glencoe and Ardgour — 2 vols.; Cairngorms Area — 2 vols.; Northern Highlands — 3 vols.; Skye — 2 vols.; Arran; Arrochar Ben Nevis.

## ACCOMMODATION:

**The Charles Inglis Clark Memorial Hut** is situated at 2,200 ft. beneath the great cliffs of the north-east face and close to the burn in the glen of the Allt a'Mhullinn (M.R. NN168723). It is perfectly placed just above the convergence of the two main approach tracks and at the divergence of the routes into the corries. Its situation is magnificent and as a base from which to climb it is unrivalled in the British Isles. Owned by the Scottish Mountaineering Club, it is available to members of B.M.C. affiliated clubs but bookings should be made through club secretaries. 16 places (minimum booking 3 places). Custodian: G. S. Peet, 6 Roman Way, Dunblane, Perthshire.

The C.I.C. Hut is the ideal centre but is becoming increasingly popular and it may be impossible to secure bookings. In this event there are two reasonable alternatives:—

**Glen Nevis S.Y.H.A.** is situated on the south bank of the River Nevis about three miles from Fort William, at the start of one of the two main approach routes.

**Steall Hut** in Upper Glen Nevis (M.R.NN 178684) is owned by the Lochaber M.C. and has 15 places. Bookings should be made to the Custodian: T. Coxfield, 'Stobhan', Fassifern Road, Fort William.

Both of these are well over 2 hours from the cliffs and in order to accomplish any really worthwhile climbing one must be fit, enthusiastic and prepared to make an 'alpine' start. They are, however, much better alternatives than camping, either in Glen Nevis or in the Allt a' Mhuilinn glen. The latter is certainly not to be recommended.

## APPROACHES

There are two standard approaches to the C.I.C. Hut:—

**1.   The route from the North-west** starts from the distillery near Lochy Bridge. (M.R. NN 125 757). Cross the main-line railway and after over half-a-mile of boggy heathland reach another, narrow-gauge, railway track. This is followed to the north for a few hundred yards until, after crossing a small bridge, a path leads up the slope on the right, through the trees. Serving as a sobering signpost, 'Dead Man's Bogey', a small sinister trolley, is usually parked at the junction between railway track and footpath. Above this point the path is quite steep and sometimes vague (there are two variations) but trends diagonally leftwards across the slope to meet the Allt a' Mhuilinn where it is dammed (i.e. just over the brow of the hill). Pass over the dam and continue up the glen for about 3 miles by a well marked track, recross the burn to link up with the other route just short of the hut and where the burn from Coire na Ciste joins the main stream.

This is probably the best and fastest approach. However it is often very boggy after a thaw, in which case the second route is preferable. In reasonable conditions and assuming that a load is carried, it should take 2—3 hours, but heavy drifted snow can make for very hard going

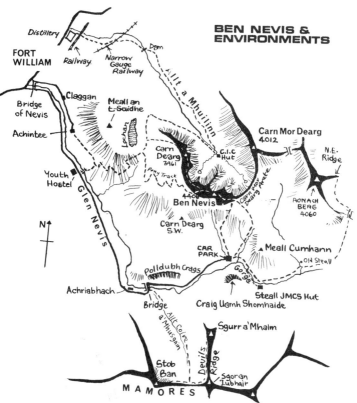

and may double the time. In bad visibility care should be taken to avoid passing the hut and continuing up into Coire Leis.

**2. The approach from the South-west** follows the zig-zagging pony-track (the tourist track to the summit of the Ben) as far as the broad saddle between Meall an t-Suidhe and the main massif of Carn Dearg N.W. Ben Nevis. The pony-track starts from Achintee Farm but a popular short-cut is to cross the bridge opposite Glen Nevis Youth Hostel and climb steeply up to join the main track. Above the saddle, which holds the large Lochan Meal an t-Suidhe (or 'Half-way Lochan'), the pony-track veers back to the right (south) crosses the Red Burn, and zig-zags up the long slope to the summit plateau. Where the pony-track swings to the south, the route to the hut branches off north-wards. It follows an indefinite path contouring the lower slopes of

13

Carn Dearg above the Half-way Lochan for about half-a-mile until it reaches the remains of an old fence on the lip of the Allt a' Mhuilinn glen. From this point it gradually descends for about 100 feet in a north-easterly direction and then continues traversing south-east across the hillside until it reaches Allt a' Mhuilinn. A large boulder, the Lunching Stone, will be seen on the left of the path along this traverse. The route now follows the right bank of the Allt a' Mhuilinn burn until it is joined by another large stream coming in from the right (out of Coire na Ciste). This is crossed and the hut, situated on the crest of a blunt spur between the streams, is about a hundred yards above.

Starting from the Youth Hostel, this approach is only slightly longer than the route up the glen but in bad visibility the route-finding is more difficult and after a big snowfall the saddle and traverse into the glen are very prone to heavy drifting.

3.   **Other approaches to the North-east face.** There are two alternative variations (with little to choose between them) starting from the large car park at the end of the Glen Nevis road. Both are exceptionally steep and are unsuitable for use as a means of reaching the C.I.C. Hut and not recommended for reaching the majority of climbs. But in good visibility for the fit valley-based climber, they give the quickest approach to the Little Brenva Face or the normal route on North-east Buttress.

(a) From the car park take a diagonal line up the hillside to reach the saddle between Meall Cumhan and Ben Nevis and then follow the ridge in a north-westerly direction. Finally, when the steep ridge merges into the easier angled slopes above, veer slightly right to gain the Carn Mor Dearg Arête at the Abseil Posts. Descend by the Posts into Coire Leis (2—2½ hrs.).

(b) Climb straight up above the car park following the right bank of the waterslide of Allt Coire Eoghainn. Once over the lip of the Coire, head up to the right (north-east) to join the previous route on the ridge a few hundred feet below the Carn Mor Dearg Arête.

(c) **From the Steall Hut** the best way is to join route (a) at the Meall Cumhan saddle. Follow a small indefinite track which leaves upper Glen Nevis immediately above the entrance to the gorge and makes a rising traverse above it, crossing the flank of Meall Cumhan, until it is possible to strike up to the saddle. Alternatively one may follow the Allt Coire Giubhsachan (above the ruin of old Steall) and head directly up the westward branch corrie to gain the C. M. D. Arête. However, there are great areas of slab in this corrie which can be very difficult under icy conditions.

## DESCENTS

Often, particularly on Ben Nevis, the descent may call for more concentration and shrewdness of judgement than any other part of the day. The best descent will be determined not only by your point of arrival on the summit plateau but the weather and snow conditions. The shortest way will not necessarily be the best and in really bad

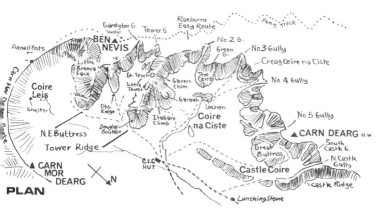

**PLAN**

conditions the only safe way off the mountain may be by route (a) below, long and tiresome though it may be. Careful use of map and compass and the sketch-plan of the cliffs given in this guidebook will suffice to get you down but local knowledge is invaluable. When visibility is good, make a close study of the general topography of the mountain and if possible visit the summit plateau with a view to memorising its details.

The ruined Observatory is an unmistakable landmark on the summit itself even though the neighbouring triangulation point, numerous cairns and the emergency shelter may be obliterated in a hard winter. From the Observatory the top of the N.E. Buttress is 300 yds. to the east of north and the top of Tower Ridge is 250 yds. to the west; this part of the Plateau is comparatively level. In order to follow the northern rim of the summit plateau, north westwards from the Observatory, one must first move in a southerly direction to avoid the deep re-entrant of Gardyloo Gully. Shortly beyond this are the heavy cornice of Tower Gully and then the projection on the top of Tower Ridge. Then there is a gradual swing back to the left and a steady descent to the top of No. 3 Gully and its characteristic pinnacle which divides the exit into two forks. The top of No. 3 Gully is about half-a-mile away from and 500 ft. below the Observatory. Now there is a slight rise and a projection to the north. This is Creag Coire na Ciste with its three gully cornices comparatively close; the last gully, North Gully, has a pinnacle which must not be confused with the one at the top of No. 3 Gully. The slope has already begun a gradual descent before North Gully's cornice is passed and it is only a short distance to the col between Ben Nevis and Carn Dearg N. W. and the wide fan cornice above No. 4 Gully.

This route along the cliff-tops is the most important part of any

15

descent in bad visibility. Beyond the shallow, indefinite col and the top of No. 4 Gully the slope at the cliff edge rises gradually once more, swinging rightwards out over the Trident Buttresses before pulling back to the head of No. 5 Gully, close to the top of Carn Dearg N. W. There is another survival shelter 250 yds. from this summit on a bearing of 200°. (G.R.NN 158719). The following are the main routes of descent:

(a)   Follow the rim of the plateau north-westwards to reach the col then descend the slope to the west where one is gradually funnelled into the gully of the Red Burn. Follow this carefully **(do not glissade)**, there may be rock bluffs to be avoided to its junction with the pony-track. Follow the pony-track down to Glen Nevis or cut over the saddle to the Allt a' Mhuilinn and the C.I.C. Hut.

(b)   Follow the above route along the cliff tops to descend by No. 3 Gully (be sure you have identified it correctly) or, **preferably by No. 4 Gully.** The latter is by far the best descent to the north; it has recently been marked by an indicator pole and generally the cornice is not so big nor the angle so steep as No. 3 Gully.

(c)   The descent from the Observatory to the C.M.D. Arête and thence down Coire Leis is the most treacherous on the mountain. Despite numerous recent aids to safety it can only be recommended in good weather and even then the initial slope is often subject to very heavy icing and may require great care. **Do not attempt this descent in bad visibility.** From the C.M.D. Arête one may descend into Coire Leis by the line of abseil posts or reverse approach route 3 into upper Glen Nevis.

A worthwhile extension (in good weather) for parties returning to the C.I.C. Hut is to follow the crescent-shaped Arête to the Summit of Carn Mor Dearg (4012 ft.) enjoying magnificent views of the Nevis cliffs. In good conditions it is occasionally possible to glissade effortlessly from the summit for nearly 2,000 ft., almost down to the Hut. But, as always with glissading, considerable caution should be exercised.

**EMERGENCIES**

There is a third emergency shelter 150 yds. above the Lochan in Coire Leis and about 400 yds. north-east of the lowest abseil post (G.R. NN174713) like the others, near the Observatory and Carn Dearg N.W. it is painted orange for easy identification. The shelters, No. 4 Gully marker and abseil posts have all been installed by the Lochaber Mountaineering club who, with the police, constitute the local rescue team. Their contributions toward accident prevention are highly commendable and it is to be hoped that users of this guide will respect their efforts and observe every safety precaution. However, genuine accidents do happen:—

There are three rescue kits available, at the C.I.C. Hut, at Steall Hut and in Fort William.

The nearest telephones are at Glen Nevis Youth Hostel or a public telephone booth near the distillery at Lochy Bridge (the number of the police station is Fort William 2361).

## GENERAL TOPOGRAPHY

The northerly faces of Ben Nevis and Carn Dearg N.W. form one continuous complex of cliffs which attain a maximum height of 2,000 ft. and extend for two miles overlooking the upper part of the Allt a' Mhuilinn glen. It is the most impressive mountain face in the British Isles. The incomparable classic ridges are flanked by formidable walls leading back into deeply recessed corries which themselves contain numerous large buttresses and gullies. The scale is so vast that it is difficult to appreciate, particularly on first acquaintance.

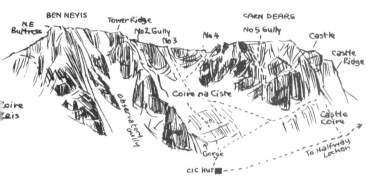

Walking up the glen of the Allt a' Mhuilinn, the first thing the climber will see on his right is Castle Ridge and its flanking North Wall. Beyond this and at a higher level is the recess of Castle Corrie which contains the Castle itself, its two demarcating gullies and to the left of these the tapering pillar of Raeburn's Buttress. The cliffs then jut out again. The left-hand side of the Castle Corrie is known as the North Wall of Carn Dearg; this cliff connects with a 1,000 ft. prow of compact rock, a truncated spur, the Great Buttress of Carn Dearg. Waterfall Gully is the dividing line between these last two. Round the corner of the Great Buttress is No. 5 Gully, set at a reasonable angle but almost 2,000 ft. in length. Ledge Route comes out of No. 5 Gully to gain the crest of the ridge at the top of the Great Buttress and follows this to the summit of Carn Dearg. To the left (east) of the Great Buttress the cliffs fall back to form the great ampitheatre of Coire na Ciste, the floor of which, at over 3,000 ft., is over a quarter mile wide. There are three relatively easy exits from the head of coire: No. 4 Gully (hidden) on the right; No. 3 Gully apparently the lowest col in the centre and No. 2 Gully which disappears to the left of the prominent buttress of the Comb. Tower Ridge is the next main feature and is one of the most important on the mountain. Narrow and very ling, it projects for half a mile from the summit plateau into the glen to terminate abruptly as the Douglas Boulder. From the foot of the Boulder (700 ft. in itself!) there is a vertical rise of over 2,000 ft. before the junction with the plateau.

To the east of Tower Ridge is the long slope of Observatory Gully which branches in its upper quarter to form Gardyloo and Tower Gullies. Observatory Gully, broad in its lower part and tapering as it rises for 1,500 ft. is only an approach to other climbs and can be regarded almost as a deep corrie. Rising to the l. of the gully are some of the most formidable climbs on the mountain: The Minus Gullies and Buttresses and the Orion face (all on the flank of North East Buttress); Zero Gully which lies in the corner between Orion Face and the long spur of Observatory ridge and finally Point Five Gully and Observatory Buttress.

The final great ridge almost at the head of the glen is called the North East Buttress. It is again a massive projection, almost 2,000 ft. in vertical height, but is steeper and therefore not as long as Tower Ridge. Below the First Platform it terminates in a great rock nose not unlike the Douglas Boulder. The Allt a' Mhuilinn glen ends in Corrie Leis below the col of the Carn Mor Dearg Arête. Overlooking this corrie is the east flank of the North East Buttress; now generally referred to as the "Little Brenva" Face.

The climbs are described from east to west (l. to r.), corrie by corrie.

_____

# CLIMBS FROM COIRE LEIS

Coire Leis is the basin at the head of the Allt a' Mhuilinn glen. From the C.I.C. Hut follow the right bank of the burn until opposite the lowest rocks below the First Platform North East Buttress, then traverse up the r.h. side of the corrie beneath the east face (about 1 hr. from the C.I.C. Hut.)

Although all the routes on the Little Brenva follow fairly arbitrary lines they are very popular. The face is alpine in character, receives the full benefit of any sun and consequently often becomes heavily iced. Generally the climbs are long and give some interesting route-finding; considerable difficulty may be experienced in misty conditions.

**Bob-run.** 400 ft. Grade II. 1½ hrs. I. Clough, D. Pipes and Party. 10th Feb., 1959. Commences almost at the level of the col of the Carn Mor Dearg Arête and follows a couloir in the l. extremity of the face. A good introduction to the more serious routes. Start to the r. of a buttress and climb 100 ft. of ice or iced rocks to gain the couloir.

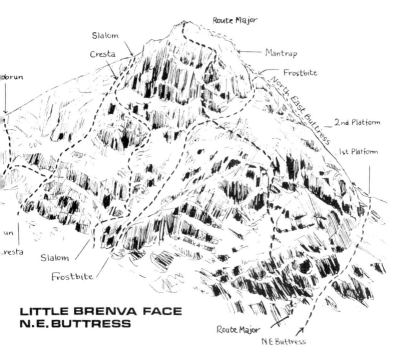

Route Major

Slalom

Cresta

Mantrap

Frostbite

bbrun

North East Buttress

2nd Platform

1st Platform

un

resta

Slalom

Frostbite

**LITTLE BRENVA FACE**
**N.E. BUTTRESS**

Route Major

N E Buttress

After another 100 ft. the route curls round to the l. by either of two variations, both of which generally give at least one further pitch on ice.

**Cresta Climb.** 900 ft. Grade II/III. 3 hrs. T. W. Patey, L. S. Lovat and A. G. Nicol. 16th Feb., 1957. The main feature of this route is a 600 ft. shallow couloir which commences above and to the l. of a 300 ft. rocky Spur and finishes amongst the small cliffs at the exit from the highest part on the l.h. side of the face. The original start was from the r. but it is now more usual to commence to the l. of the rocky spur and about 100 ft. r. of Bob-run. 100 ft. of icy rocks (or ice) are climbed to gain a long broad snowshelf. A small gully leads up from the r.h. side of the shelf to reach the couloir proper which is followed to its termination in an ice basin. Traverse up to the r. to gain an easy snow slope which leads out to a finish about 50 yds. from the top of N.E. Buttress.

**Slalom.** 900 ft. Grade II/III. 4 hrs. D. Pipes, I. Clough, J. M. Alexander, R. Shaw and A. Flegg. 6th Jan., 1959. The upper part of

19

the r.h. side of the face is a steep rock wall, the Central Spur. Both Slalom and Frostbite start in a bay below this wall and to the right of a 300 ft. rocky spur.

Slalom starts up a shallow tongue of snow from the l. of the bay and zig-zags up through rock bluffs towards the middle of the wall of the Central Spur. Below the Spur a long rising leftwards traverse is made to gain an easy snow slope which leads to the foot of a rocky ridge overlooking the couloir of Cresta. The rocks usually give the crux of the climb and lead to the final easy exit slope which is shared with Cresta.

**Frostbite.** 900 ft. Grade III. 6 hrs. I. Clough, D. Pipes, J. M. Alexander, P. A. Hannon and M. Bucke. Feb., 1958. Starts from the above-mentioned bay and follows an icy groove up to the right to gain a 400 ft. snowfield. Follow this rightwards and cross a rocky ridge below the nose of the Central Spur proper to gain further snowslopes slanting rightwards under the Spur. These eventually lead out onto the crest of the N.E. Buttress below the Mantrap. On the first ascent this gave formidable problems.

**Route Major.** 1,000 ft. Grade III. 3/5 hours. H. MacInnes and I. Clough 16th February, 1969. This route follows the line of The Eastern Climb and provides one of the most enjoyable winter routes on Ben Nevis. Start from above and to the l. of North East Buttress Route and follow the ice ribs up the wall to gain a snowslope crossed by Frostbite. Cross this and continue up the buttress above by a chimney line going up and right (complicated route finding). Where the route goes close to the Mantrap, break out left on a horizontal traverse then up various small snowfields to the top.

**North East Buttress.** 1,500 ft. Grade III/IV. 4/10 hrs. First Winter ascent unknown. The normal winter route avoids the rocks below the First Platform by going up into Corrie Leis until a broad easy shelf leads back up to the r. to the First Platform. Shortly above the Platform the rocks on the crest become very steep and the easiest route is to traverse an exposed ledge on the r. until a gully leads back up to the l. to reach the small Second Platform. Alternatively the steep step may be turned on the l. or even taken direct. Above the Second Platform the ridge is followed, turning obstacles, until a smooth blunt 15 ft. nose bars the way. This is the notorious Man-trap which can be extremely difficult in icy conditions. It is best turned on the r. by a slight descent and traverse to a scoop. This leads to the foot of a steep corner which again can be very hard. It may be best to move slightly down and to the l. until, not far above the top of the Man-trap, a shallow chimney leads up to the l. of the ridge crest on to easier ground. This upper part of the route is normally the crux of the climb and can be exceptionally trying, but the major difficulties are relatively short and it is not too far to the top; probably better to force the route (although even combined tactics have sometimes been of no avail) than to be faced with the long retreat.

# CLIMBS FROM OBSERVATORY GULLY

**Slingsby's Chimney.** 400 ft. Grade II/III. 1-2 hrs. Climbed in summer 1895. First winter ascent unknown. A direct approach route to the First Platform of N.E. Buttress from the west, useful as an alternative to the easy shelf from Coire Leis or as a climb in itself, for doubtful weather or poor conditions. To the r. of the slabby rocks of the nose leading to the First Platform is an obvious shallow gully fault. This gives the climb. The sloping shelf gives a fast descent from the First Platform into Coire Leis.

**Platforms Rib.** ´420 ft. Grade IV. 6 hrs. H. Macinnes, I. Clough, T. Sullivan and M. White. 8th March, 1959. To the r. of Slingsby's Chimney is another, longer, well-defined gully (Minus Three Gully). Commences in the gully and follows the rib on the l. to an overhang which may require direct aid. Above this the route goes r. to use a section of Minus Three Gully before moving back l. to a groove which leads out onto the crest of the N.E.B. not far above the First Platform.

The big bay above and to the r. of Minus Three Gully and to the l. of Observatory Ridge harbours some of the most ferocious ice climbs in Scotland. These routes brought standards of difficulty much in advance of anything previously achieved. After the passage of ten years, experts still regard them with considerable awe and they give a challenge and inspiration for the future. **Suitable only for the most expert of ice-climbers.**

R. of Minus Three Gully is Minus Two Buttress. The next buttress is the tall, cigar-shaped, Minus One Buttress. Between these buttresses is a thin gully which only becomes pronounced in its upper part.

**Minus Two Gully.** 900 ft. Grade V. 8 hrs. J. R. Marshall, J. Stenhouse and D. Haston. 11th Feb., 1959. Formidable, unrepeated and probably technically the hardest of the Nevis gullies.

R. of Minus One Buttress is Minus One Gully and then the great Orion Face with Zero Gully following the huge ice corners on its r.

**Orion Face.** 1000 ft. Grade V. 12 hrs. Robin Smith and R. K. Holt. Jan., 1959. Follows more or less the summer line of the Long Climb as far as the Basin and then traverses up to the crest of the N.E.B. which it gains well below the Man-trap. Unrepeated

**Orion Face Direct.** 1500 ft. Grade V. 8 hrs. under exceptional conditions. Robin Smith and J. R. Marshall. 8th Feb., 1960. A magnificent "diretissima" line which goes straight up to the Basin by steep ice grooves and continues with little deviation to the summit. Unrepeated.

**Zero Gully.** 1500 ft. Grade V. 5 hrs. in superb conditions. H. MacInnes, T. W. Patey and A. G. Nicol. 18th Feb., 1957. The lower 400 ft. of this climb is excessively steep and good belays are hard to find, making it an unusually serious undertaking. The first ascent was justly recognised as "a truly great achievement in the history of ice climbing." It has been repeated on several occasions but never in such favourable conditions; the average time taken on subsequent ascents is about 10 hrs.

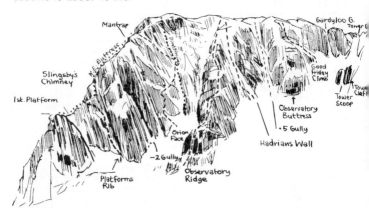

**Observatory Ridge.** About 1200 ft.. Grade III/IV. 4-14 hrs. H. Raeburn, F. S. Goggs and W. A. Mounsey. April, 1920.

Often considered to be the finest and most difficult of the classic ridges, the line of the route generally follows the crest of the ridge. The lowest buttress normally gives the most serious problems. The easiest winter line is to gain a shelf on the l. flank and about a third of the way up this buttress and then work obliquely rightwards to the crest. Above this, difficulties can be turned and the upper part of Zero Gully may offer an easier alternative for the last 500 ft.

**Hadrian's Wall.** 800 ft. Grade V. 5 hrs. W. D. Brooker, J. R. Marshall and T. W. Patey. 1st Feb., 1959. On the steep, slabby West Wall of Observatory Ridge in the vicinity of a long smear of ice. It gave 500 ft. of sustained difficulties of the highest order (involving a diagonal abseil at one stage) but eased off higher up. Unrepeated.

**Point Five Gully.** 1000 ft. Grade V. 7-29 hrs. J. M. Alexander, I. Clough, D. Pipes and R. Shaw. Jan.. 1959. Lies in the corner formed by the flanks of Observatory Ridge and Observatory Butturess. The controversial first ascent was made when the climb was "out of condition" (i.e. continued hard ice) and took 29 hrs. of climbing spread over 5 days! The second ascent, by R. Smith and J. R. Marshall, took only 7 hours in good conditions. The few subsequent repetitions have taken much longer and one ascent involved a bivouac.

**Good Friday Climb.** 500 ft. Grade III. 3-4 hrs. G. G. Macphee, R. W. Lovel, H. R. Shepherd and D. Edwards. 7th April, 1939. The start of the climb is about 1½ hrs. from the C.I.C. hut, at the head of Observatory Gully and below Gardyloo Gully. On the l. a snow shelf leads out to the top of Observatory Buttress and then a gully is followed for about 250 ft. until it is blocked by a wall. The route now goes r., then back l. up another gully system which eventually leads out to the plateau very near the summit. The upper part is steep and intricate and can be very hard in icy conditions.

**Gardyloo Gully.** 350 ft. Grade II/III. 1½-2 hrs. G. Hastings and W. P. Haskett-Smith. 26th April, 1897. One of the most popular winter routes on the mountain, the l. fork and direct continuation above Observatory Gully. Normally a straightforward snow slope as far as a great chockstone, about 100 ft. below the cornice. Sometimes there is a tunnel beneath the chockstone which leads to a short, steep ice pitch on the r of the chockstone, but in an exceptional winter the whole route may be one uniform slope. The cornice can be difficult and is sometimes double.

**Smith's Route** (Gardyloo Buttress) 400 ft. Grade V. 6½-12 hours. R. Smith and J. R. Marshall, 8th February, 1960. Gardyloo Buttress is on the immediate r. of the gully and this formidable route uses the prominent slanting grooves which come from the upper funnel. Climb a groove to the lower end of the main grooves where there is a peg belay, 120 ft. Cross the lower groove by traversing diagonally l. Easier ground is ascended until one is forced to the r. and up on steep ice to the l. edge of the upper groove which is followed to the funnel. Easier then, by the funnel to the top. Unrepeated.

**Tower Gully.** 700 ft. Grade 1. 1 hour. G. Hastings, E. L. W. & W. P. Haskett-Smith. 25th April, 1897.

A broad snow shelf leads from the foot of Gardyloo Gully rightwards, below the Buttress and above a 300 ft. band of lower rocks, to the gully proper. This is easy but the cornice is sometimes very large and may even need tunnelling.

**Tower Cleft.** 250 ft. Grade III. 3½ hrs. G. Pratt and J. Francis. 17th Feb., 1949. A deep slit between the walls of Tower Ridge and the 300 ft. band of rocks which cut off the direct approach to Tower Gully. It is a unique subterranean ice climb giving several short steep pitches but is probably not feasible without an exceptional banking of snow.

**Tower Scoop.** 200 ft. Grade III/IV. 3 hrs. I. Clough and G. Grandison. Follows an obvious line up the middle of the 300 ft. rock band below Tower Gully. A steep ice pitch gives entry to a runnel of ice which terminates in a bulge.

**The Tower Ridge.** 2000 ft. vertically and half a mile. Grade III. 4-8 hrs. J. N. Collie, G. A. Solly and J. Collier. 29th March, 1894.

This, the most famous of the great Nevis ridges, is a magnificent expedition. Technically easier than the N.E. Buttress or Observatory Ridge, it should not be underrated. The main difficulties are concentrated high up and the whole route is exceptionally long and arduous.

# BEN NEVIS

Route Major — Gardyloo Gully — Tower Gully — Great Tower — No 3 Gully — No.2 Gully — No 3 G.Butt. — Comb Gully — Slalom — Cresta — Bobrun — Little Brenva Face — Tower Scoop Cleft — The Comb — Observatory Buttress — Garadh na Ciste — Coire Leis — Slalom — Frostbite — 1st Platform — Observatory Gully — Coire na Ciste — Route Major — North East Buttress — Observatory Ridge — Tower Gully — Observatory Ridge — Douglas Boulder — Tower Ridge

The normal winter route avoids the face of the Douglas Boulder by going round into the bottom of Observatory Gully and then cutting back to the r. above a bay to follow the easy East Gully to the Douglas Gap. Alternative starts are the Douglas Boulder Direct or the Douglas Gap West Gully. A 60 ft. groove leads from the gap to the ridge which rises gently and becomes quite narrow. A short steep wall is climbed by using a rightwards slanting ledge and then a series of short rises lead to another gentle section. Beyond this is the Little Tower (really only another steep step) which is climbed by starting on the l. Extreme care should be exercised on this section; a fall over the l. side of the ridge (Echo Wall) can result in the climber being unable to regain contact with the rock.. The great Tower, a 100 ft. wall blocking the ridge, is not far above. Immediately below it, the Eastern Traverse follows a narrow and exposed ledge to the l. Round the corner is a chimney formed by great fallen blocks and above this steep rocks with good holds lead to the summit of the Tower. The route then descends slightly to the Tower Gap, goes down into it and ascends the little wall beyond. The short connecting ridge finally leads up to merge with the summit plateau which is best gained by the snow slope on the r.

**Douglas Boulder Direct.** 700 ft. Grade II/III. 1½-3 hrs. W. Brown, L. Hinxman, H. Raeburn and W. Douglas. 3rd April, 1896. Takes the front face of the Boulder from the lowest rocks. This should be regarded as a climb in its own right, particularly useful for a short day.

24

# CLIMBS FROM COIRE NA CISTE

From the C.I.C. Hut there are several approach routes into Coire na Ciste (see diagram). Average time to the start of the higher climbs is about 1 hr. A long bluff of broken rocks and slabs guards the lip of the corrie. On the left they are penetrated by a gorge but early In the season this may have a big pitch in its upper part. It is probably better to start up the bluff about 100 yds. to the r. by a shallow gully or groove which leads to easier ground. On the extreme r. of the bluff is an approach by an indefinite gully or start by aiming straight up towards the Great Buttress of Carn Dearg and walking up a gully to the broad easy slope below No. 5 Gully. This slope leads back leftwards above the rock bands into the coire. Yet another approach (the best for reaching the first four climbs) is on the extreme l. of the corrie, close under the cliffs of the Douglas Boulder and above and l. of the gorge.

**Douglas Gap West Gully.** 450 ft. Grade I. 1 hr. from the C.I.C. Hut. Much steeper than the E. Gully but is straightforward and, for a fit party, is slightly the faster route to Tower Ridge.

**Vanishing Gully.** 350 ft. Grade IV/V. R. Marshall and G. Tiso, 1961. This little-known but important climb starts over 100 yds. along the slope from Douglas Gap W. Gully and beyond a big bay reaching into the flank of Tower Ridge. The gully, scarcely even a scoop in its lower section, becomes more definite as it rises. Hard from the start,

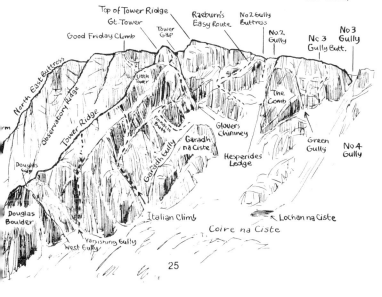

it steepens into formidable bulges towards the top of the difficult section (about 400 ft. in all). It emerges onto a big snowfield and an exit can be made to the Crest of Tower Ridge well below the Little Tower.

**The Italian Climb.** 600 ft. Grade IV. 4 hrs. J. R. Marshall, A. Mac-Corquodale and G. J. Ritchie. 1958. Continuing along beneath the W. side of Tower Ridge one comes to a deep gully bounded on the l. by a prominent two-tier rib. The Italian Climb follows the gully which gives two major ice pitches and then a diagonal traverse across the face to the r. to gain the crest of Tower Ridge below the Little Tower.

**Garadh Gully.** 300 ft. Grade II/III. 1-3 hrs. Starts just above and r. of Italian Climb and separates the steep little buttress of Garadh Na Ciste from Tower Ridge.

To the r. of the Garadh and above the exit of the gorge approach a long snowslope tapers up between the flanks of Tower ridge and the prominent conical buttress of the Comb, to terminate as No. 2 Gully. This slope is the approach for the next 8 climbs.

**Pinnacle Buttress of the Tower.** 500 ft. Grade III. 4-6 hrs. D. J. Bennet and A. Tait. 17th Nov., 1957. Starting from the top of Garadh na Ciste, a broad shallow gully is followed to the l. for about 150 ft. before traversing r. along a ledge above overhanging rocks and beneath the steep crest of the Buttress. Beyond the crest the rocks are more broken, and the climb now follows a series of snow grooves in the r. flank until it is possible to move leftwards to the top of the Buttress. Follow a ridge to the foot of the Great Tower and traverse r. until a line of chimneys can be followed to the top of it.

**Glover's Chimney.** 450 ft. Grade III/IV. 6-8 hrs. G. G. Macphee, G. C. Williams and D. Henderson. 17th March, 1935. Starts above Garadh na Ciste and follows a long couloir leading to a chimney below the Tower Gap. The entry is made by an ice-fall, often over 100 ft. high and very steep, usually climbed from l. to r. The final chimney is the crux. More than 120 ft. of rope is useful as it is difficult to find suitable stances. The climb finishes in the Tower Gap.

**Raeburn's Easy Route.** 350 ft. Grade II. 2 hrs. S.M.C. party. April, 1920. Some distance above the previous routes, above the start of Comb Gully (on the r.) and just before No. 2 Gully narrows. A very long and slightly rising traverse is made leftwards out of the No. 2 Gully approach and across a large snowslope. Aim for the point where the crags above peter out and climb a 100 ft. ice pitch (relatively low angled) to gain a great snow shelf below more crags. This leads back to the r., gently rising, until a shallow gully gives access to the plateau.

**No. 2 Gully Buttress.** 400 ft. Grade II/III. 2 hrs. J. R. Marshall, L. S. Lovat and A. H. Hendry, 23rd March, 1958. Immediately to the l. of No. 2 Gully. Steep snow and occasionally iced rocks lead to a shelf below a vertical upper wall. A short but difficult ice pitch on the l. leads to easier ground.

**No. 2 Gully.** 400 ft. Grade I/II. 1½ hrs. J. Collier, G. Hastings and W. C. Slingsby. Easter 1896. Hardest and possibly the most interesting of the easier gullies Above the introductory slopes it becomes a deep slit. Generally a straightforward but steadily steepening slope, it can (especially early in the season) offer an ice pitch and the cornice is often quite difficult.

**Comb Gully Buttress.** 450 ft. Grade III/IV. 5 hrs. J. M. Alexander and I. Clough. 8th Jan. 1960. A large ice column normally forms on the right wall, beyond the start of Comb Gully and before the narrowing to No. 2 Gully proper. The route starts below this and climbs. slightly rightwards, to gain a large snow basin. A groove leading from the l. h. side of the basin is followed by a rightwards rising ramp. This leads into the upper half of a very prominent curving chimney, the crux of the climb and an awkward exit on the l.

**Comb Gully.** 450 ft. Grade IIII/IV. 2-8 hrs. F. G. Stangle, R. Morsley and P. A. Small. 12th April, 1938. The obvious gully running up the l.h. side of the Comb. Since Dougal Haston climbed it solo in 20 minutes. its reputation has declined. However, it is still a serious route and 2 hrs. is a fast time in excellent conditions. Early in the season it may be particularly hard with continuous steep ice in the upper half and even later in the year its condition is very variable.

**Hesperides Ledge.** 200 ft. Grade III. 3 hrs. J. R. Marshall, J. Stenhouse and D. Haston. 12th Feb. 1959. Follows the lower 250 ft. of Comb Gully and then a relatively easy but highly spectacular steep curving shelf which leads rightwards across the wall to the crest of the Comb.

**Green Gully.** 400 ft. Grade IV. 4-8 hrs. J. H. B. Bell, J. Henson, R. Morsley and P. A. Small. 4th April 1937. The line of demarkation between the Comb and No. 3 Gully Buttress. Despite the passage of time, this climb still holds its reputation. It invariably gives two big ice pitches.

**No. 3 Gully Buttress.** 400 ft. Grade II/III. 2 hr. L. S. Lovat and D. J. Bennet. 18th Feb. 1957. A bold rock buttress projects into the corrie on the l. and below the narrowing to No. 3 Gully. About two thirds of the way up it, is an obvious large platform; the first objective. Start in a big snow bay below the prow of the buttress and climb to reach the platform. Grooves then lead up to the l. and a steep corner gives a fine finish. The upper part of the route is magnificently exposed.

**No. 3 Gully.** 300 ft. Grade I. About 2 hrs. from the C.I.C. Hut to the plateau. First ascent dates back to pre-1870. The angle of the approach slope gradually increases as it rises from the basin of Coire na Ciste and by the time it narrows to a gully proper, it is quite steep. No pitches but the final section is divided by a pinnacle rib, that on the l. being the easier.

**South Gully, Creag Coire na Ciste.** 400 ft. Grade II/III. 1-2 hrs. G. G. Macphee. 10th April 1936. Starts high on the l. h. side of Creag Coire na Ciste and just below No. 3 Gully proper Use an obvious ramp slanting diagonally to the r. This leads to an ice pitch which gives entry to a steep final funnel. Cornice is often difficult.

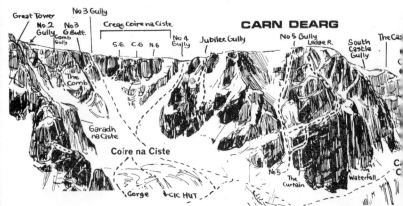

**Central Gully.** 600 ft. Grade III. 2 hrs. I. Clough and J. M. Alexander. 27th January 1959. Starting from the lowest part of the crag, snow-Slopes are followed to the l. of a rocky rib to reach the l.h. of two parallel ice chimneys which cleave the steep central wall. This is climbed for 120 ft. before crossing to the r.h. gully which leads into the final corniced funnel.

**North Gully.** 370 ft. Grade II. 1½ hrs. J. Y. Macdonald and H. W. Turnbull. 24th March, 1934. This, the r.h. and most obvious of the three gullies on this cliff, starts (to the l.) from the foot of No. 4 Gully. The lower section of the gully almost always holds an ice pitch but its length may vary from 10 to 100 ft. The narrow lower section leads to a wide easier-angled slope which is followed obliquely rightwards to the cornice.

**No. 4 Gully.** 350 ft. Grade I. About 2 hrs. from the C.I.C. Hut to the plateau. The easiest winter route on Ben Nevis and the best descent on the N. face. It curls gently round to the r. between the cliffs of Creag C. na Ciste and the S. Trident Buttress. Its exit is very wide so that, even given a heavy build-up of cornice, it should be possible to find an easy weakness.

**Jubilee Gully.** 800 ft. Grade II/III. 2-4 hrs. K. Bryan and L. S. Lovat. 11th March, 1956. Lies in the back of the recess below and r. of the S. Trident Buttress and is not far above (and r. of) the floor of the main corrie. Shortly after the start the gully bifurcates—take the l. fork. It contains one main ice pitch. Above, a huge basin of snow gives a choice of routes.

**No. 5 Gully.** 1600 ft. Grade I. About 2 hrs. from the C.I.C. Hut to the summit of Carn Dearg N.W. Lies between the Trident Buttresses and the Great Buttress of Carn Dearg and commences below and well to the right of the main basin of Coire na Ciste. It is a straightforward snow climb. Above a small pitch the gully narrows, and then opens into a huge funnel. The normal route keeps to the r., to exit near the top of Carn Dearg.

**Ledge route.** 1900 ft. Grade I. About 2½ hrs. from the C.I.C. Hut to summit of Carn Dearg N.W. An interesting excursion. Starts up No. 5 Gully but leaves it by a rightwards rising ramp shortly after it becomes a gully proper. The ramp leads out above the top of the Curtain onto a broad, almost horizontal ledge which fades out to the r. Before the ledge narrows, leave it by a leftward slanting gully which comes out onto a broad sloping snowshelf. This shelf gives an easier but less interesting start; it comes out of No. 5 Gully and slants easily up to the r. to a large platform and cairn at the summit of the Great Buttress of Carn Dearg. A large pinnacle block, a useful landmark, is passed just before rounding the corner to reach the platform. The route now follows the ridge until another large cairn marks the top of No. 5 Gully Buttress. A further connecting ridge leads on up to the summit of Carn Dearg N.W. **In good weather** this route gives a more interesting, if slower, descent than the gullies. The ridge should be followed down to the top of Carn Dearg Buttress and then the broad highest shelf (marked by the pinnacle block at the start) can be followed easily into No. 5 gully. Instead of descending the gully (which may have a small pitch in it), continue to the far side where a similar broad shelf leads gradually down between two buttresses to easy slopes below all the cliffs.

**The Curtain.** 300 ft. Grade IV/V. 6½ hrs. J. Knight and D. Bathgate. Feb., 1965. There is a large slab corner in the upper l.h. side of the l. flank of the Great Buttress of Carn Dearg which, in winter, develops into a great cataract of ice—a difficult technical problem.

---

# CLIMBS FROM CASTLE CORRIE

The best approach from the C.I.C. Hut to the Castle Corrie is to follow the little gully leading through the rock bluffs immediately below No. 5 Gully. Make a rising rightwards traverse below the Great Buttress and the N. Face of Carn Dearg to the foot of the Castle. This point may also be reached by leaving the path between the Lunching Stone and the C.I.C. Hut and cutting straight up into the corrie by way of another gully.

**Waterfall Gully.** 700 ft. Grade III/IV. 7 hrs. D. Pipes, I. Clough, J. M. Alexander, R. Shaw and A. Flegg. 8th Jan., 1959. The obvious gully immediately r. of the Great Buttress. The 150 ft. entry is generally an ice pitch, exceedingly steep in the lower part. Thereafter the gully is straight-forward to an awkward slabby exit into the large basin below the summit buttresses and gullies of Carn Dearg. If time is pressing, the easiest way off is up to the left to join Ledge Route.

**North East Face Route**. 800 ft. Grade III/IV. 5 hrs. H. Brunton and J. Clarkson. 14th Feb., 1957. In the far l.h. corner of the Castle Corrie is a gully, the common start for this route and Raeburn's Buttress/Intermediate Gully. Follow it to the foot of a big ice pitch and then a shelf on the l. wall leads onto a ledge at the top of a large flying buttress (Cousins' Buttress). The ledge, quite wide but possibly banked with snow to a high angle, is followed horizontally leftwards for about 200 ft. before climbing a 200 ft. icefall, at first, steep and extremely exposed but thereafter the angle decreases and the large basin below the summit buttresses and gullies of Carn Dearg is reached.

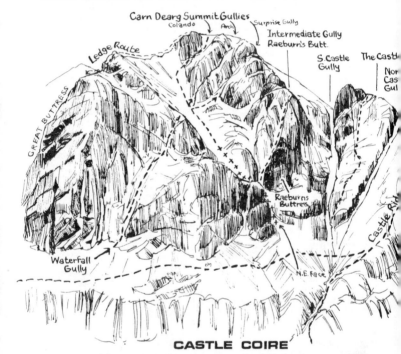

**CASTLE COIRE**

**Carn Dearg Summit Gullies.** These form a logical continuation to the previous climb. They may also be reached by descending into the basin from the large cairn on Ledge Route. Climbed by I. Clough, P. S. Nicholson and D. Pipes on 8th and 12th April, 1958.

**Colando Gully.** 600 ft. Grade I. ½ hr. 8th April, 1958. The l.h. gully. Straight-forward.

30

**Arch Gully.** 600 ft. Grade I. $\frac{1}{2}$ hr. 8th April, 1958. The central gully marked by a huge block which forms the Arch at about half height. Straight-forward but steep.

**Surprise Gully.** 600 ft. Grade I/II. 1 hr. 12th April, 1958. The shallow r.h. gully leads by broken rocks to a shoulder and to the top by an ice groove on the l.

**Arch Buttress.** 600 ft. Grade II/III. 3 hrs. D. Pipes and A. Flegg. 3rd Jan., 1959. Between Arch and Colando gullies. After 150 ft. on the crest, the route follows a groove on the right then easier climbing to some difficult chimneys.

**Surprise.** 600 ft. Grade III. 4 hrs. I. Clough and B. Halpin. 3rd Jan., 1959. On the buttress to the r. of Arch Gully, following the crest as closely as possible to a steep wall above the Arch block. A 100 ft. rightwards traverse below this wall is followed by short awkward walls leading back slightly l. to a small ledge about 30 ft. above the traverse. A move downwards and to the r. gives entry to a steep 120 ft. corner which gives a strenuous final crux pitch.

**Raeburn's Buttress/Intermediate Gully.** 700 ft. Grade III/IV. 3$\frac{1}{2}$ hrs. W. D. Brooker and J. M. Taylor (by the buttress finish) and R. H. Sellers and J. Smith (finishing by Intermediate Gully). 31st January, 1959. G. G. Macphee and party had previously made 1st ascent of the gully in April, 1938 but perhaps not under true winter conditions.

Raeburn's is the tall thin buttress above the l.h. corner of the Castle Corrie. It finishes as a slender tapering arête to the l. of which is the prominent narrow Intermediate Gully. The start is the same as for Face Route; the gully leading up into the l.h. corner of the corrie. After about 200 ft. an obvious chimney line on the r. leads up to a cave and then the route takes the r. wall to reach the foot of Intermediate gully. There is a cave exit at the top of the gully which is otherwise straightforward. The crest of Raeburn's Buttress proper is immediately to the r. of the foot of the gully. It narrows to a sharp blade at the top but this may be turned by a corner on the r.

**South Castle Gully.** 700 ft. Grade I/II. 1-2 hrs. W. Brunskill, W. W. King and W. W. Naismith. 1st April, 1896. The long gully between Raeburn's Buttress and the Castle. Normally an easy snow climb. One small pitch may be particularly difficult early in the season; climbed by a gangway on the l. wall.

**The Castle.** 700 ft. Grade II/III. 3 hrs. W. Brown, J. Maclay, W. W. Naismith and G. Thomson. April, 1896. In summer an awkward bulging little wall guards the base. This may be hard in winter but more probably it will be entirely obliterated by an avalanche cone. The route then goes straight up. The upper rocks are climbed by means of a gully, slabs, a chimney and a further shallow gully all in the centre of the buttress, to beneath the final very steep wall. The route now goes up to the r. over snow-covered slabs, to the top. Great care should be taken on the slabby sections which are very prone to avalanche.

**North Castle Gully.** 700 ft. Grade I/II. 1$\frac{1}{2}$ hrs. J. H. Bell and R. G.

Napier. 4th April 1896. The gully bounding The Castle on the r. Steeper than S. Castle Gully, it contains several short easy chockstone pitches, often completely covered giving a straight-forward snow climb.

**Castle Ridge.** 1000 ft. or more. Grade II. 2-3 hrs. J. N. Collie, W. W. Naismith, G. Thomson and M. W. Travers. 12th April, 1895. A good safe climb under most conditions, by far the easiest of the classic ridges. The most usual start is by a little r.-slanting gully leaving Castle Corrie just below the start of N. Castle Gully. It may however be started much lower down. This increases the length to about 1,500 ft. and gives more continuous difficulties. By the normal start, the rocks of the ridge crest immediately above the little gully give the only unavoidable difficulty. Above this, the best sport is had by keeping to the r.

---

## CLIMBS ON THE NORTH FACE OF CASTLE RIDGE

**The Serpent.** Over 1000 ft. Grade II. 2 hrs. I Clough, D. Pipes and J Porter. 12th Feb. 1959. The easiest of the three routes on the North Face of Castle Ridge. No technical difficulty but serious, with route-finding problems. Above and to the l. of the Lunching Stone a small r.-slanting gully gives access to a wide shelf which curves up to the r After 500 ft. this leads into a couloir which slants, still rightwards, steeply up the face to come out on the shoulder of Carn Dearg.

**Nordwand.** 1,400 ft. Grade II/III. 4 hrs. I. Clough, D. Pipes, B. Sarll, F. Jones and J. Porter. 11th Feb. 1959.

A fine mixed route which is often in condition when higher climbs are not. Technical and route-finding problems similar to those on the Little Brenva face but no sunshine; a genuine, grim, nordwand atmosphere. Starts fairly well up to the r. of the centre of the face at a slight bay. A long vertical snow-filled trench on the screes below the face often shows the way. Nordwand follows a short gully up the face for 80 ft. and climbs an ice pitch before moving l. (or works diagonally l. below the ice pitch). It continues to follow the easiest way up the centre of the wall crossing the couloir of the Serpent and continuing by snowfields to the steep summit rocks. An awkward l. rising traverse leads to the top.

**La Petite.** 600 ft. Grade III. 3 hrs. D. Pipes and I. Clough. 11th Feb., 1959. The climb starts about 100 ft. r. of Nordwand and goes up steeply for 120 ft. to gain entry to a couloir. This entry will generally give an 80 ft. ice pitch and then ice glazed rock. The couloir, which leads obliquely r. (not obvious from below), should give two more good ice pitches before finishing on the Carn Dearg shoulder.

---

# OUTLYING CLIMBS IN THE BEN NEVIS REGION

**Steall Gully.** 700 ft. Grade II. 1-2 hrs. First ascent unknown. This is on the S.E. slope of Ben Nevis, just to the S. of and commences a little below the col between Meall Cumhann and the Ben. The approaches from the car park at the end of the Glen Nevis road and from Steall Hut converge below this gully before carrying on up to the col and the Carn Mor Dearg Arête. The climb is quite variable but can give some interesting pitches of no great difficulty. Its chief merit is its accessibility from Glen Nevis.

**Climbs on Stob Ban.** (3274 ft.) The N.E. face of Stob Ban is steep and rocky with three main buttresses. This area provides the only real climbing in the Mamores and there is a path up the the Allt Coire a' Mhusgain from Glen Nevis. The buttresses and the gullies between them give several possibilities, (Grade I-II). From the summit the best return route to Glen Nevis is to follow the ridge round to Sgurr a' Mhaim (3601 ft.). Descend to the E. following the ridge to the col at the head of the Allt Coire a' Mhusgain (where one can descend to Glen Nevis by the same path used in approach) and climb to the summit of next top to the west (Sgor an Iubhair, 3,300 ft.; unnamed on the O.S. map). From this peak there is almost a mile of ridge, quite narrow, often heavily corniced and leading over an elegant subsidiary top to the summit of Sgur a' Mhaim. This last spectacular section is known as the Devil's Ridge.

**The North-east Ridge of Aonach Beag** (4,060 ft.). 1,500 ft. Grade II/III. 3-5 hrs. J. Maclay, W. W. Naismith and G. Thomson. April, 1895. A fine climb but remote and very rarely done. From the Steall Hut, however, the approach is not unreasonable (about 3 hrs.). The path through Upper Glen Nevis may be followed beyond the ruin of old Steall for a mile or so before cutting up to reach the col between the eastern top of Aonach Beag and Sgurr Choinnich Beag. Descend slightly into the Allt a' Chul Choire and contour N.W. for about a mile to reach the start of the climb. The lower section is not particularly difficult but the middle section is quite narrow, with several pinnacles and gives good situations. It may be quite hard in icy conditions. Higher up it becomes broader and easier and finishes about 60 yds. to the N.W. of the summit.

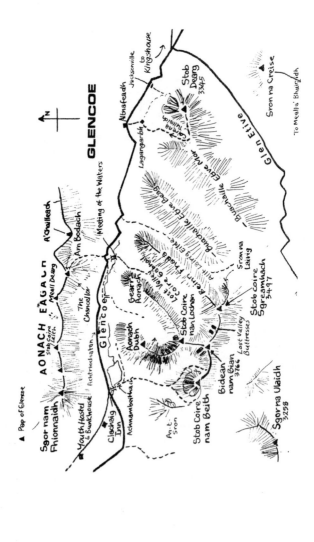

GLENCOE

N

▲ Pap of Glencoe

Sgor nam Fhionnaidh
Youth Hostel & Bunkhouse

AONACH EAGACH
Stob Coire Leith
Meall Dearg
A'Chailleach
The Chancellor
Am Bodach
Achtriochdan
Meeting of the Waters
Clachaig Inn
Achnambeithach
An t-Sron
GLENCOE
Stob Coire nan Lochan
Gear Aonach
Aonach Dubh
Coire Gabhail
Bein Fhada
Allt Lairig Eilde
Stob Coire Sgreamhach 3497
Sron na Lairig
Lost Valley Buttresses
Bidean nam Bian 3766
Stob Coire nam Beith
Sgorr na Ulaidh 3258

Jacksonville
to Kingshouse
Altnafeadh
Lagangarbh
Stob Dearg 3345
Coire na Tulaich
Buachaille Etive Mor
Lairig Gartain
Buachaille Etive Beag
Blackmile
Glen Etive
Sron na Creise
To Meall a' Bhuiridh

# GLENCOE

## ACCOMMODATION

Accomodation in the Glencoe area is all in the valley but, unlike Ben Nevis, this does not matter since neither the climbs or the approaches are so long or arduous. There are three hotels; the Glencoe and the Kingshouse at either end of the glen and the Clachaig Inn on the Glencoe old road. Also on the old road (about half a mile west of Clachaig and adjoining each other) are the Youth Hostel and the privately owned Bunk-house. There are also several huts in the glen belonging to various Scottish clubs. At least two of them are generally available to members of B.M.C. affiliated clubs. Camping is another possibility but it is far better to have drying facilities.

**Lagangarbh.** The S.M.C. hut beneath the 'Buachaille' (M.R. NN 221560). 18 places. Bookings must be made through club secretaries from custodian: A.C.D. Small, 36 Clarence Drive, Glasgow, W.2.

**Black Rock Cottage.** Owned by the Ladies' Scottish Climbing Club and situated beside the access road to the White Corries Chair Lift, one mile S.E. of the Kingshouse Hotel (M.R. NN 268530). 10 places to be booked through club secretaries from custodian: Miss P. Cain, Ayton House, Glenfarg, Perthshire.

**Emergencies**

The first call in the event of accident or a party overdue should always be made on the Glencoe Mountain Rescue Assn.:— Hamish MacInnes, Allt-na-reigh (the white cottage in the middle of the glen above the Meeting of Three Waters)—Tel: Kingshouse 225. Rescue kits are kept here and at Glencoe Police Station (phone Ballachulish 222 or dial 999). A Police Mountain Rescue team works in co-operation with the civilian team. Lagangarbh Hut has no telephone but there is one at Altnafeadh on the main road and at most other private dwellings in the glen. There are public 'phones at Kingshouse and Clachaig and a telephone box beside the main road at the Glen Etive junction.

———————————

# CLIMBS ON STOB DEARG, BUACHAILLE ETIVE MOR
## (3345 ft.)

Buachaille Etive Mor is a long ridge with four tops. Stob Dearg is the north top, a beautifully symmetrical cone as seen from the junction of the roads leading down into the glens of Etive and Coe. Of the four tops it is the highest and the only one which gives much climbing and it is generally referred to as The 'Buachaille'. It is the best rock climbing peak in Glencoe but its winter climbing potential is very limited, mainly due to its relatively low altitude.

The better routes are all on the central section of the mountain —see diagram for details.

Most of the climbs start from the Crowberry Basin—below Crowberry Ridge and Gully and contained by the lower parts of Curved Ridge and North Buttress.

The most usual starting point is from Altnafeadh on the main road (parking available in several neighbouring laybys). The River Coupall is crossed by a bridge leading to Lagangarbh. Beyond the hut, a track leads south-eastwards, gradually rising, to cross the foot of Great Gully after about a mile. From this point one can take a steep short cut by following the easy lower part of North Buttress and bearing left into the basin below Crowberry Ridge. Alternatively one can continue following the track below North Buttress, which rises slowly to meet the 'Jacksonville' approach below a prominent Waterslide slab. The Jacksonville approach starts from a parking place (concealed entrance) on the south side of the main road about a mile to the east of Altnafeidh. It descends to the river where stepping stones lead to the square black hut on the far side. This is Jacksonville, property of the Creag Dhu M.C. (guests by invitation only). The track leads across the moor and directly up to the Waterslide. The disadvantages of this, the shortest approach, are that the stepping stones may be covered or icy and that the descent route leads down to Lagangarbh. From the Waterslide junction, the path zig-zags up to the start of D Gully Buttress and then makes a rising traverse to the r., keeping close up against the cliffs, to come out finally in the bottom of the Crowberry Basin (about 1-1½ hrs. from Lagangarbh).

**Descent.** There is only one reasonable descent route in winter. From the summit follow the fairly level ridge for 300 yards to the S.W. then change course to descend due west for about ¼ mile to reach a shallow cairned col at the head of Coire na Tulaich (more usually called Lagangarbh Corrie). This section can be particularly difficult in white-out conditions. There are occasional cairns but it may be necessary to stay roped up and take both front and back bearings to keep on course. The most common mistake is to continue too far S.W. and descend into Glen Etive. This slope is not too difficult but it is a long walk back on the road. Care should also be taken not to stray too far to the N. or W. or to turn W. too early as there are some large crags in the head of Coire na Tulaich. From the col a steep initial slope leads down into the corrie. This slope is often in a hard icy condition and it may be best to wear crampons and to belay. Even in soft conditions it is better not to glissade as there are often boulders and screes exposed lower down. There have been many accidents here. The lower part of the corrie (there is a track down the l.h. side if the snow of the lower gully is deep) leads easily down to Lagangarbh and the road.

**D Gully Buttress.** 800 ft. Grade III. 3 hrs. to Curved Ridge. The normal approach path passes under the foot of the buttress. It is narrow and defined by the deep D Gully on the r. and, on the l. by indefinite rocks marging with Central Buttress with which it makes a right angle. The start of the buttress is vague and entry is usually made from the foot of D Gully. A prominent steep smooth step high up the buttress is a useful landmark. The first few hundred feet of the buttress are fairly easy but then the way is blocked by the steep smooth step. Turn on the l. by a shallow chimney and gully leading back rightwards to regain the crest, very narrow at this point. Above, a long slabby section gives the crux, usually climbed near its r. edge. After a further 100 ft. or so the buttress ends on a shoulder whence a r. traverse should be made to gain Curved Ridge and Easy Gully. Either continue the ascent or descend, using the easiest combination of these two routes. This route is useful for giving a relatively short day.

**D Gully.** 800 ft. Grade II. 2 hrs. May be no more than a straight-forward snow slope (Grade I) but more usually it will give up to four short pitches. Traverse r. to Curved Ridge/Easy Gully at the top. Not very good but useful in bad weather.

**Curved Ridge/Easy Gully.** Over 1000 ft. Grade II (but can attain Grade III after heavy snowfall). 2-4 hrs. G. T. Glover and R. G. Napier. April, 1898. A magnificent route to the summit of the mountain, it passes through grand rock scenery, is a good general viewpoint and gives interesting climbing under almost any conditions. Certainly the most useful winter climb on the Buachaille and can be quite hard.

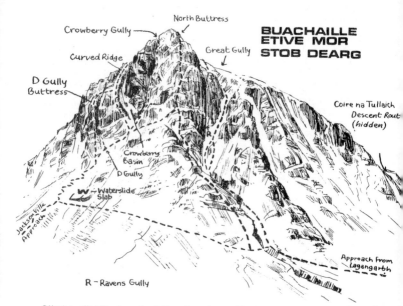

Climbs slightly l. out of the Crowberry Basin by any of several variations (the crest of Curved Ridge proper or any of the gullies and grooves in this area) and passes beneath the Rannoch Wall of Crowberry Ridge to reach a final big cairn, at the top of Curved Ridge proper and below the foot of Crowberry Tower. From the cairn a horizontal l. traverse for about 100 ft. brings one onto a snowslope with two wide gully exits. The gully slanting back to the r. reaches the Crowberry Tower Gap and from there a short groove leads l. then r. to the top of Crowberry Gully and the final summit slopes. The gully going up slightly leftwards leads directly to the summit rocks. It is probably the quickest but not the most interesting way. If time permits, an ascent of the Crowberry Tower can be included if the first route is followed; from the gap a short corner is climbed to a ledge on the l. when an easy rising spiral traverse leads to the top. There are more interesting routes up the Tower but this is the easiest and the best in descent.

**Crowberry Ridge by Garrick's Shelf.** 800 ft. Grade IV. 4-10 hrs. W. M. Mackenzie and W. H. Murray. March, 1937. Probably the hardest pre-war route and a significant break-through; the start of modern Scottish ice climbing. Scenic and historic interest and still a tough climb which requires special conditions. The Shelf is really a steep ramp on the r.h. side of (and set back from) the crest of the Crowberry

Ridge. It is immediately l. of Crowberry Gully and the easiest way of reaching the start is to follow the gully for 100 ft. or so before going out to the r. to gain the foot of three adjacent chimneys. The r. wall and rib of the middle chimney is usually the best way of gaining the Shelf ramp which itself is divided by two big rock ribs. The route uses the scoop and rib on the r. The crucial section is normally near a small pinnacle on this rib; it may be impossible to turn it on the r. and a l. traverse may also be extremely difficult. Beyond the pinnacle a long continuation scoop or groove leads to the easy upper section of the ridge below the Crowberry Tower. The ridge leads on to the summit of the Tower but if time is pressing it may be quicker to traverse l. beneath the Tower to gain the easy gullies leading up above the big cairn on Curved Ridge.

**Crowberry Gully.** Over 1,000 ft. Grade III/IV. 4-8 hrs. W. M. Mackenzie, J B. Russell, J. F. Hamilton and J. K. W. Dunn. 9th Feb., 1936. A magnificent classic climb of considerable quality. Unfortunately it is not often in good condition and can be dangerous due to avalanches. Conditions can vary remarkably and can change in a short space of time. In easy conditions it may be completely banked up with snow except for an ice pitch at the Junction (where a rightwards rising traverse is made from the foot of the deeply recessed Left Fork) and another at the exit from a cave near the top of the gully. The cave pitch will usually give the crux of the normal route (although the Junction pitch can also be quite hard), climbed by the r. wall which is invariably of green ice and 30 to 40 ft. in height. If attempted when 'out of condition' (particularly early in the season) there may be many more pitches and the Junction and Cave pitches may be all-but-impossible with only a thin veneer of verglass.

**Crowberry Gully, Left Fork.** Grade IV. C. M. G. Smith, R. J. Taunton and I. C Robertson. 18th March, 1949. The Left Fork leads steeply out of the main gully to the Crowberry Tower Gap. The deeply recessed gully soon becomes a narrow iced chimney which is capped by a large overhanging block. The capstone will always be exceptionally difficult but good protection is available. Although it is a hard technical problem, this fork is very short and shouldn't require as much time as a complete ascent by the normal route.

**North Buttress.** Over 1,500 ft. Grade III. 2-5 hrs. First winter ascent not recorded but for an account of an early ascent of this route (and several others used in this guide) see **Mountaineering in Scotland** by W. H. Murray. The lower part of the buttress is easy and has already been referred to as an approach to the Crowberry Basin. The steep rocky upper section can be relied upon to give a good climb in almost any conditions. The route is variable but the line most generally followed in winter is by a series of chimneys to the l. After about 400 ft. these lead out onto easier angled slopes but higher rock steps can still give considerable difficulty in icy conditions.

**Great Gully.** About 2,000 ft. Grade I/II. 2-5 hrs. Norman Collie. 1894. In some conditions the lower part of Great Gully can give a series of fine little ice pitches. However, it is usually entered by traversing in after ascending several hundred feet by North Buttress's lower slopes. The upper section rarely gives more than an easy snow climb but the scenery is most impressive and the climb is worthwhile for this alone.

**Raven's Gully.** 600 ft. Grade V. 3-8 hrs. H. MacInnes and C. J. S. Bonington. 14th Feb., 1953. The dark slit high up on the North Buttress wall of Great Gully. The climb is a formidable technical problem. There may be up to eleven pitches, most of them hard and some requiring direct aid and cunning rope manoeuvres. **Direct Finish.** Y. Chouinnard and D. Tompkins, Feb. 1970. This is a very serious finish to the gully. Follow up under chockstone near top of gully. Hard straddling on iced rock to finish on original route just under top of gully. Grade V.

---

## CLIMBS FROM COIRE GABHAIL (THE LOST VALLEY)

Starting from a layby on the s. side of the road, a path leads down to the footbridge over the River Coe near the Meeting of Three Waters. It continues up into the corrie, first through a gorge and eventually crossing the stream and passing through a boulder-field to reach the floor of the corrie, a flat half mile of shingle and grass. The walk so far is very interesting and is worthwhile for its own sake on an off-day. At the entrance to the corrie floor is the 30 ft. Boulder—a useful landmark. Beyond the corrie floor there are two paths to the r. of the stream and at different levels. The highest is the better of the two and makes a gradual ascent along the side of the valley until the stream is crossed above its deep gorge bed. The track disappears soon above this point and the two main approach/descent routes bifurcate. One route continues straight ahead to the col at the end of the valley—between Stob Coire Sgreamhach, 3,497 ft., on the l. (unnamed on the O.S. map) and Bidean nam Bian. The slope is easy but there may be fairly large cornices. The other route bears r., keeping r. of the r.h. tributary stream, into a subsidiary corrie which leads up to the col between Bidean and Stob Coire nan Lochan. Either of these are good descents but care may be required near the cornices. The cliffs of Stob Coire nan Lochan may also be reached by bearing back in a northerly direction, beyond the cliffs of the Upper East Face of Gearr Aonach, obliquely across the hillside to reach the shoulder where the Gearr Aonach ridge rises steeply towards the summit of Stob Coire nan Lochan. Allow 1½-2 hrs. in ascent by any of these routes.

## BEINN FHADA AND STOB COIRE SGREAMHACH

The western flanks of the Beinn Fhada ridge and the culminating summit of Stob Coire Sgreamhach offer numerous possibilities for climbing, mainly at about Grade I-II standard. The alpine-like face of Sgreamhach can be particularly interesting, giving elementary route-finding practice and avoidable, ice pitches. There is a rocky step where the Beinn Fhada ridge joins up with Sgreamhach. In descent. turn difficulties on the r. of this section and leave the crest of the Beinn Fhada ridge about a third of a mile beyond the North-east Top (3.064 ft.) at a col marked by cairns. Do not continue to the Nose but descend steeply into Coire Gabhail or, on the r., into the Lairig Eilde.

## LOST VALLEY MINOR BUTTRESS

The smaller and l.h. of the two prominent buttresses at the head of the valley and below the middle of the ridge leading up from the col to Bidean.

**Left-hand Gullies.** 300 ft. Grade I. $\frac{1}{2}$ hr. To the l. of the buttress are two easy gullies separated by a rocky rib.

**Chimney Route.** 250 ft. Grade III/IV. 2-3 hrs. R. Marshall and J. Moriarty. Jan. 1959. The obvious deep chimney to the l. of the centre of the face. A series of chockstone pitches can give considerable difficulty.

**Central Scoop.** 250 ft. Grade III/IV. 2/3 hours. I. Clough and Mrs. N. Clough. Feb. 1969. This is the chimney line between Chimney Route and Right Edge. The chimney (short) starts from a platform some 40 ft. up and the route takes this corner/chimney, then follows the buttress to the top.

**Right Edge.** 300 ft. Grade III. 2 hrs. J. R. Marshall, J. Stenhouse and D. Haston. Feb., 1959. At the r.h. side of the face a broad snowfield-ramp leads up rightwards below overhangs. Access to the ramp is gained by an icy chimney below its l. end and an arête leads from the top of the ramp to the summit.

**Right-hand Gully.** 200 ft. Grade I. $\frac{1}{2}$ hr. Probably Glencoe School of Winter Climbing parties. The gully immediately to the r. of the buttress gives a straightforward but steep climb and often has a large cornice.

## LOST VALLEY BUTTRESS

The large r.h. buttress is in two distinct sections; an easier angled l.h. portion but very steep and set back at a higher level on the r.

**Left-hand Gully.** 300 ft. Grade I. $\frac{1}{2}$ hr. Probably G.S.W.C. parties. The gully is bounded on the l. by a broken indefinite rib of rock. Straightforward climbing to a steep corniced exit.

**Sabre Tooth.** 400 ft. Grade III. 2-3 hrs. I. Clough and H. MacInnes. 9th Feb. 1969. There is a prominent, vertical, 150 ft. corner towards the r. h. side of the l.h. section of cliff. This has been climbed but gives an artificial and much more difficult start which would elevate the general standard of the climb to Grade IV. Starting to the l. of the corner, the route goes up into a recess and breaks out rightwards, eventually arriving on a terrace above the big corner. The terrace leads back l. to the foot of a steep shallow 40 ft. corner (good belays on the l.). The corner is hard for a climb of this standard but well protected.

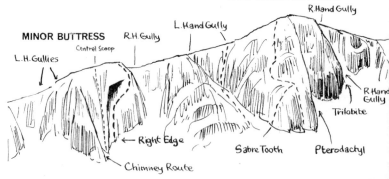

**LOST VALLEY BUTTRESSES**

Above it, a line of grooves is followed to the top.

**Pterodactyl.** (Moonlight Gully). 350 ft. Grade IV. 10 hrs. H. MacInnes and D. Crabbe. Jan., 1964. Follows the line of the shallow gully lying in the corner which divides the two sections of cliff. The overhanging entry to the upper couloir is extremely difficult—one of the hardest technical problems in the area—but relatively short. The route follows a steep corner to a stance beneath the overhang which projects for six feet, then climbs to gain the upper couloir using the crack to the l. of the main icicle formation. Unrepeated.

**Trilobite.** 200 ft. Grade II/III. 1-2 hrs. H. MacInnes and I. Clough. 9th Feb., 1969. On the side wall of the buttress, leaving the r.h. gully where it begins to narrow and opposite a ramp which goes up steeply out to the r. Trilobite follows a very steep groove which runs directly up the gully wall to the top of the buttress.

**Right-hand Gully.** 300 ft. Grade I/II. 1 hr. Probably G.S.W.C. party. A steep gully with a big cornice, often containing a small ice pitch. About 100 ft. up, below the steepening and narrowing to the pitch and level with the runnel of Trilobite, is a variation sloping steeply up to the right—**The Ramp** (Grade I/II).

## EAST FACE OF GEARR AONACH

These climbs are all on the r.h. side of Coire Gabhail beyond the Lost Valley Boulder. Particularly useful when conditions are poor at higher levels and for their relatively short approach. However, many of them are fine climbs in their own right and some rank with the best in Glencoe. Icy conditions are preferable. The best descent is by the Zig-zags on the Nose of Gearr Aonach (described under Stob Coire

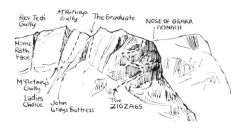

nan Lochan). They are best described from r. to l., as one sees them in walking up the valley:—

**The Graduate.** 500 ft. Grade III/IV. 5 hrs. D. A. Knowles, J. Loxham. D. Wilson and A. Wilson. 8th Feb., 1969. The boulder-field which blocks the entrance to the floor of the Lost Valley is the result of a great landslide which has left a huge deep recess in the cliffs of Gearr Aonach. Follows the great r. angled corner at the l.h. side of this recess and is most easily reached by going up and slightly rightwards from the Lost Valley Boulder.

**Ingrid's Folly and Peregrine Gully.** 100 ft. Grade II. 2-3 hrs. Probably G.S.W.C. party. The foot of Ingrid's Folly is only about 5 minutes walk diagonally up the slope to the s. of the Lost Valley Boulder. It is a well-defined gully tucked away in a corner, much better than its appearance might suggest. The long grassy buttress to its r. (and immediately l. of The Graduate) is **John Gray's Buttress**, Grade II. Ingrid's Folly consists of several relatively easy rock pitches which give good sport when veneered in ice and there is a particularly interesting through-route. Above the last pitch, where the gully gives an easy slope to the top, a 100 yds. traverse to the l. leads into Peregrine Gully. This gives further pitches; another cave with a through-route and an easy passage below a gigantic block which forms an archway just before the steep exit.

To the l. of Ingrid's Folly and Peregrine Gully the cliffs of Gearr Aonach give broken crags in the lower half leading to an almost continuous wide horizontal terrace. Above the terrace are a series of steep walls, unpleasantly grassy in summer but which give good winter climbing. The first big break in these upper cliffs is a large rightward facing corner—McArtney Gully. The next climb is on the r. wall of this corner and shares the same approach, threading through the lower crags to the terrace.

**Lady's Choice.** 500 ft. Grade III. 3½ hrs. A. Fyffe and Niki Clough. 14th Feb., 1969. Follows a groove line which curves up to the r. and then back l. to finish in a steep chimney with a chockstone.

**McArtney Gully.** Grade II/III. 500 ft. 2 hrs. H. MacInnes and G.S.W.C. party. 3rd Feb., 1969. The lower half of this big corner gully is reasonably straight-forward but the upper part is very steep. A vertical chimney is followed to a diagonal groove and corner which give the crux.

**Frostbite Wall.** 680 ft. Grade IV. 4/6 hours. H. MacInnes, A. Gilbert, P. Debbage, D. Layne-Joynt, D. Allright. Feb. 1969. Take the main line of the ice ribbon up wall, gaining it first by a rightwards traverse from the bottom of it, then back l. to it some 150 ft. up via a ledge. Climb the ice ribbon direct to top. N.B.—This route is usually in condition when the ice ribbon is complete from top to bottom of cliff.

**Frostbite Groove.** 670 ft. Grade IV. 3/5 hours. H. MacInnes and G.S.W.C. Feb. 1969. At the point where Frostbite Wall traverses back across obvious ledge, take the ice chimney/groove line up and slightly r. Break out l. after one pitch, over ice bulge to gain ice scoop. Climb scoop and small chimney to top.

**Rev. Ted's Gully.** 1,000 ft. Grade II/III. 2-3 hrs. H. MacInnes & Rev. Ted    ?  Follows the long and obvious couloir which slants leftwards up the full length of the face, some distance l. of McArtney Gully. The lower ice pitches are usually avoided on the r. and a variety of finishes are available although the direct continuation is probably the best and most difficult.

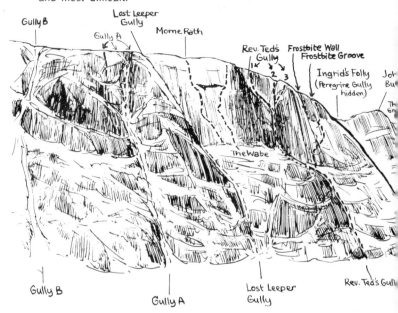

**EAST FACE · GEARR AONACH**

Given the right conditions the upper cliffs to the l. of Rev. Ted's Gully give some of the most sensational ice climbing in Glencoe. The terrace below the upper wall can be reached by the lower sections of Rev. Ted's or Lost Leeper Gullies. The upper wall (Upper East or Mome Rath Face) has high up, a long barrier of overhang. In hard conditions much of the face becomes masked with smears of ice and the overhang is decorated with a fantastic fringe of icicles which can attain 30 to 40 ft. in length. There are two winter routes on the wall, passing either side of the icicle fringe.

**The Wabe.** 450 ft. Grade IV. 5½ hrs. I. Clough, H. MacInnes and J. Hardie. 16th Feb. 1969. Approximately follows the line of a prominent icefall to the r. of the icicle fringe. A short wall is climbed. Belay on a snow ledge above the main terrace. The route then goes up slightly to the r. before making a long diagonal leftwards traverse across the icefall towards a prominent nose and a stance at 150 ft. After passing below the nose (immediately above an overhang) the route veers r. then l. to reach a pedestal stance below the r. edge of the icicle fringe and then moves back r. to climb the icefall where it passes through a recessed panel. Good stance on the r. above this section. The final pitch goes diagonally r. and then back l. The route is sustained throughout and extremely exposed.

**Mome Rath Route.** 500 ft. Grade IV. 4½ hrs. A Fyffe and J. McArtney. 16th Feb., 1969. The general line of the route is a long leftward slant. It starts below the icicle fringed overhang by an obvious broad ramp and continues the line up to the l. into a chimney. This is followed for about 60 ft. before going l. again into another chimney which leads to a bay. A slabby iceplated rib on the l. is followed by a short steep corner-chimney. Again, this route combines sustained technical climbing with a high degree of exposure.

**Lost Leeper Gully.** 1,000 ft. Grade III. 3 hrs. H. MacInnes and G.S.W.C. party 13th Feb., 1969. The shallow indefinite gully which comes down immediately to the l. of the Mome Rath Face and reaches the lower slope of the valley above the gradually rising path. The route weaves its way up through the lower crags, giving interesting routefinding, and the more distinct upper gully should give at least two good ice pitches.

**Gully A.** 800 ft. Grade III/IV. 4 hrs. H. MacInnes and D. Crabbe. Jan., 1964. The next gully to the l. again, starting some distance beyond where the path starts rising from the floor of the Lost Valley. It runs the full height of the face, is indefinite in its lower part, deep-cut in the middle and becomes a steep straight-forward slope in the upper section. It faces south and is hidden until immediately below it. A pitch climbed on the l. leads into the gully which is followed to the r. to a bulging groove, the crux of the climb.

**Gully A (Central Branch).** 750 ft. Grade IV. 3-4 hours. D. Haston and J. Stenhouse. Jan. 1969. Gully A divides at the start of the main pitch and this variation takes a line directly up a steep ice scoop.

**Gully A (Left Branch).** 800 ft. Grade IV. 3/5 hours. H. MacInnes and G.S.W.C. party. Feb. 1970. This is the branch of the gully which starts as a very steep ice pitch slightly to the l. of the main gully A. Follow gully line throughout (escape possible halfway up on l.) and take either the chimney line above or break out r. up steep iced rock.

**Gully B.** 800 ft. Grade II. 1½-2 hrs. Probably G.S.W.C. parties. The next gully to the l. of Gully A is straight-forward except for one large chockstone pitch which may be quite hard.

**Gully C.** 800 ft. Grade I/II. 1 hr. Probably G.S.W.C. parties. A long shallow couloir on the extreme l. before the cliffs fade out entirely. It may contain a few short pitches. Competent climbers may find this route useful as an approach to Stob Coire nan Lochan.

---

# CLIMBS ON STOB COIRE NAN LOCHAN (3657 ft.)

The cliffs high of the N.E. facing corrie immediately below the summit of Stob Coire nan Lochan usually give good winter climbing even when lower level cliffs are spoiled by thaw. The floor of the corrie is at about 2,700 ft. and the cliffs, which have an average height of 500 ft., are arranged in a semi-circle below the summit and the shoulder extending northwards from it.

Probably the most attractive approach is by the ridge of Gearr Aonach. After crossing the bridge at the Meeting of Three Waters and following the track up towards Coire Gabhail as far as the beginning of the gorge section (about a half mile above the bridge), the route cuts up to the right aiming for the cliffs of the E. Face of Gearr Aonach some distance to the l. of the Nose. The route up the flank to the top of the Nose is known as the Zig-zags. Although marked by occasional cairns, the route is not too easy to follow and it is wise to try and pick it out from well below. Careful inspection will reveal two obvious slanting terraces, up to the r. and then back to the l., winding up through otherwise sheer cliff. The Zig-zags are gained by walking leftwards up a grass slope below the cliffs until the start of the first terrace is reached in a corner immediately to the r. of a 50 ft. prow of rock. After about 100 ft. of scrambling the terrace leads gently up to the r. under some steep cliffs to an easy slope which is followed for another 100 ft. or so before taking a short gully corner on the l. This leads to the second big terrace which is followed to its l.h. end. After a short ascent, another long rightwards rising traverse and a brief tack back to the l. bring one out at the big cairn at the top of the Nose of Gearr Aonach. The ridge is then followed until an easy traverse can be made into the floor of the corrie. (About 1½-2 hrs. from the road). This route is difficult to find in descent and, without prior knowledge and certainly in bad visibility, the valley route (next described) is preferable.

Although it is not so attractive from the scenic point of view, the approach by the valley leading up between Gearr Aonach and Aonach Dubh is now as fast as the previous route, due to the recent introduction of a bridge over the River Coe at G.R. NN 167567. This is gained by walking along the old road east of Achtriochtan farm for about half a mile and then descending to the river. Alternatively cars may be parked in a big layby on the S. side of the road, E. of Achtriochtan, and a descent made directly to the bridge. Beyond the bridge is a scree fan. Paths follow both sides of the valley but neither is well defined until well above the scree. The l.h. track is probably the best. This comes in from the bridge at the Meeting of Three Waters and traverses round beneath the Nose of Gearr Aonach to enter the Stob Coire nan Lochan valley about 500 ft. above the level of the scree fan of the other bridge. A long steady ascent up the valley eventually leads over the final lip to the floor of the corrie.

Other approaches are by the Lost Valley (already mentioned) and by Dinner-time Buttress on the West Face of Aonach Dubh (described later).

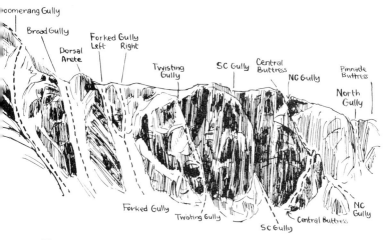

The topography of the corrie is relatively simple. Below the summit of Stob Coire nan Lochan is Summit Buttress. This name applies particularly to the steep r.h. face; the open face and broken rocks of the l. flank can be climbed anywhere at Grade I standard. To the r. of Summit Buttress are Broad Gully and Forked Gully. To the r. again are the South, North and Pinnacle Buttresses, all separated by narrow gullies.

**Boomerang Gully.** 800 ft. Grade II. 2 hrs. J. Black, R. G. Donaldson and W. H. Murray. Jan., 1949. This curls round to the l. of the steep rocks of Summit Buttress (and r. of an indefinite rocky ridge which bounds the l. flank) and swings back to finish by the ridge leading on from the top of the Buttress to the summit of the mountain. The first long tapering gully slope is followed up to the l. from the foot of the steep rocks until an entry pitch on the r., rocky and frequently iced, leads up into the main couloir. If the entry pitch is missed the initial slope leads out onto the face of the l. flank. The main couloir curves rightwards and leads to the final rocky arête.

**Scabbard Chimney.** 500 ft. Grade IV. 5 hrs. L. S. Lovat, J. R. Marshall and A. H. Hendry. 12th Feb., 1956. The obvious deep chimney which starts near the lowest rocks of the steep Summit Buttress and slants up to the r. The crux, a 'sentry box' at about 200 ft., may require the use of combined tactics and direct aid. Above the chimney, a gully on the l. leads up to the final arête.

**Broad Gully.** 600 ft. Grade I. ½ hr. A very easy route which often provides the best means of descent into the corrie but care may be required in icy conditions.

**Pearly Gates.** 500 ft. Grade II. 1 hr. I. Clough and party. 17th April, 1966. Leaves Broad Gully at about half height where the side walls of Summit Buttress become more broken and a notch or 'gateway' is seen on the l.h. skyline. Zig-zag ramps lead up to this feature in 150 ft. and after passing through the 'gates' a shallow fan of snow leads directly to the summit.

**Dorsal Arête.** 500 ft. Grade II. 1-2 hrs. J. Black, T. Shepherd, J. Allingham and J. Bradburn. 28th Jan., 1951. Starting up a sprawling mass of rocks to the r. of Broad Gully, the route becomes increasingly interesting as height is gained, finally tapering to a very narrow and well defined arête. Good rock belays and the climb is very useful in bad conditions.

**Forked Gully.** 500 ft. Left Fork: Grade I/II. 1 hr. Right Fork: Grade II/III. 2 hrs. The gully to the r. of Dorsal Arête gives a steep but normally straight-forward snow climb by the Left Fork. The Right Fork (r. of a 200 ft. rock rib which splits the upper section) is steeper and often iced.

**Twisting Gully.** 500 ft. Grade II/III. 2-3 hrs. W. H. Murray, D. Scott and J. C. Simpson. Dec., 1946. One of the classic Scottish snow climbs, this route takes a shallow gully immediately to the l. of South Buttress and is separated from Forked Gully by an indefinite rocky rib. The first 100 ft. leads up into a deep recess from which there are two continuations. The normal route follows an icy chimney on the l. until it bulges when a short l. traverse is made across the gully wall to gain the l. rib. There is an awkward mantleshelf move on the short arête which leads to easier ground. Above this crux pitch, about 100 ft. of snow leads to another short ice pitch which can be turned on the r. if necessary (this pitch may even be completely obliterated). The gully continues without difficulty to the final wide fan and a choice of steep exits.

**Twisting Gully, Right Fork.** Grade III. 3 hrs. J. R. Marshall and I. D. Haig. Jan., 1958. A more difficult and more direct variation on the middle section of the normal route. From the deep recess, a very steep pitch up an ice corner is followed by a continuation runnel (separated from the original route by a broken rib) which joins the normal route below the final fan.

**S.C. Gully.** 500 ft. Grade III. 4 hrs. P. D. Baird, L. Clinton and F. Clinton. March, 1934. The steep gully between South and Central Buttresses is another classic and a serious route requiring good conditions. Early in the season a steep ice pitch often bars entry to the gully but, if it is too formidable, the rib on the l. may give an easier alternative. Steep snow then leads up into the bed of the gully proper. The route then traverses up to the r. to gain and follow a steep ice gangway which often has a bulge shortly before the top. A long run-out will normally be required to reach a satisfactory belay above the pitch. Beyond this, steep snow leads to the cornice which may be quite difficult.

**Central Buttress.** 500 ft. Grade III. 2-3 hrs. H. Raeburn with Dr. and Mrs. C. Inglis Clark. April, 1907. Starts from a bay to the l. of the lowest r.h. spur and goes up to the r. to gain its crest. The ridge leads to a tower which is best turned on the r., regaining the crest by a short chimney. A good route with splendid situations.

**N.C. Gully.** 600 ft. Grade I/II. 1 hr. The gully between Central and North Buttresses generally gives a steep but straightforward snow climb. Early in the season it may have short pitches. A good introductory gully.

**North Gully.** 300 ft. Grade I/II. 1 hr. Divides North Buttress from Pinnacle Buttress. It is steep, sometimes gives a short pitch and often carries a heavy cornice.

**Pinnacle Buttress Groove.** 200 ft. Grade II/III. 1½ hrs. L. S. Lovat and N. G. Harthill. 5th Jan., 1958. Follows a steep groove on the North Gully flank of Pinnacle Buttress to the l. of a prominent arête. Start on the r. near the foot of North Gully. An excellent short climb in icy conditions.

**Pinnacle Buttress, North-east Face.** 300ft. Grade III. 2 hrs. I. Clough and J. R. Woods. 26th Jan., 1967. Starts at the lowest rocks and climbs up r. then l. up a short groove to a steep wall. An icy corner crack on the r. leads to a ledge and a higher ledge is gained up to the r. From the l. end of this upper ledge an awkward chimney leads to the roof of the buttress.

---

# CLIMBS ON THE NORTH FACE OF AONACH DUBH

The huge dark recess of Ossian's Cave is the big feature of the cliffs on this face and the climbs all start from Sloping Shelf, a long rightwards rising ramp below it. A long gully with numerous waterfalls slants rightwards down the hillside below and l. of the Cave. The ridge on the l. of this gully gives one possible line of approach but both bridges over the River Coe are about a mile away from its foot. The best approach is to cross by the new footbridge to the east of Achtriochtan (as for Stob Coire nan Lochan) and use a long grass rake which slants up to the r. crosses the foot of another deep gully and eventually reaches the upper part of the waterfall gully just below the point where Sloping Shelf breaks out on the r. Scramble across the gully to gain the Shelf and follow it up to the r. to the start of the climbs (about 1-1½ hrs. from the road).

**Descent.** The best descent from the top of Aonach Dubh is to go S.W. for about a quarter mile to the shallow col before the rise to Stob Coire nan Lochan, then follow the tributary stream down into lower Coire nan Lochan and cross the main stream to reach the path on its east bank. Alternatively one may descend from the col by the W. Face of Aonach Dubh using the top section of No. 2 Gully and Dinner-time Buttress but prior knowledge of the route is preferable and the Coire nan Lochan descent is certainly the safest in bad visibility.

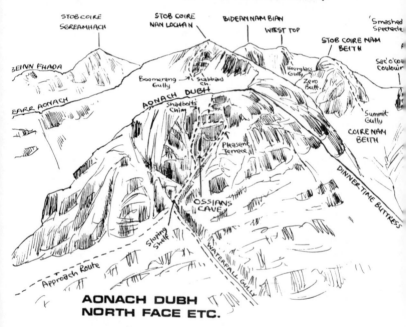

## AONACH DUBH
## NORTH FACE ETC.

**Shadbolt's Chimney.** 700 ft. Grade IV. 7 hrs. D. and R. Goldie. 13 Feb., 1955. A deep chimney goes up from Sloping Shelf not far below and to the l. of Ossian's Cave. This gives the first 150 ft. of the climb. The route then uses the grassy buttress on the r. to avoid a loose section before a difficult 30 ft. chimney leads on to an amphitheatre. A wide shallow slabby gully continues to the top. The l. wall should give the easiest route on the final section.

**Pleasant Terrace.** 800 ft. Grade II/III. 3 hrs. J. McArtney, I. Clough and party. 14th Jan., 1969. This climb and Deep-gash Gully both start from the upper r.h. end of Sloping Shelf. The Shelf itself may give difficulty in icy conditions and the best route may be to cross the shallow gully to gain the ridge to the r. Deep-gash Gully is obvious—immediately above the end of the Shelf. The entry pitches to gain the r.h. end of Pleasant Terrace proper, start from a bay to the l. of the foot of Deep-gash Gully. Two pitches lead up leftwards; the second, starting as an awkward corner crack, will generally be quite hard. The "Terrace", which soon narrows to a thin and sensational ledge, leads horizontally leftwards for several hundred feet. After a slight descent the ledge broadens again below a deep, narrow chimney which is followed, with difficulty, to the top.

**Deep-gash Gully.** 200 ft. Grade IV. J. Cunningham and M. Noon. 24th Feb., 1957. This relatively short climb contains a high concentration of technical difficulties; a 30 ft. back-and-foot pitch, a short steep ice pitch, a through-route and a pitch climbed by threading a rope through a hole in the roof of a cave and prusiking up it. The final pitch involves squeezing feet first through a small hole and then climbing an ice overhang!

---

# CLIMBS ON THE WEST FACE OF AONACH DUBH

The West Face of Aonach Dubh which faces the Clachaig Inn is a vast and complex series of buttresses and gullies. Most of the hard climbs require a good build-up of ice during a prolonged spell of hard frost but even the easier routes are worthwhile if only for the impressive rock scenery through which they pass. The buttresses are split horizontally into three tiers by Middle Ledge (between the lowest and Middle tiers) and The Rake (between the middle and upper tiers). Splitting the face vertically are six main gullies, numbered from l. to r., and there are two scoops which split the main mass of the middle tier.

The best approach is to cross the bridge at the outlet from Loch Achtriochtan, follow the track to Achnambeithach and go through a gate to the r. of the farmhouse. The fence should then be followed. eventually turning up a short open gully to the l. to begin the ascent of Dinner-time Buttress. No. 2 Gully is easily crossed at this point, giving access to the lower grass ridge of B Buttress or any of the other climbs further to the r. The safest descent is to go down into lower Coire nan Lochan (as for Aonach Dubh N. Face descent) but the quickest way, in good visibility, is by the easy upper part of No. 2 Gully and the lower part of Dinner-time Buttress.

**Dinner-time Buttress and entries to Middle Ledge.** 1½-2 hrs. Dinner-time Buttress is on the l.h. side of the face and below the col between the Nose of Aonach Dubh and Stob Coire nan Lochan. It is defined by the vague No. 1 Gully on the l. and by the deep water-course of No. 2 Gully on the r. Except for the last few hundred feet it is mainly grass with short sections of scrambling. The upper rocks may be climbed

(Grade I/II) but they are more often turned by entering No. 2 Gully which at this height is wide and easy. The route is normally used as an approach to Stob Coire nan Lochan or Middle Ledge or in descent. However, it can provide an interesting excursion in bad weather.

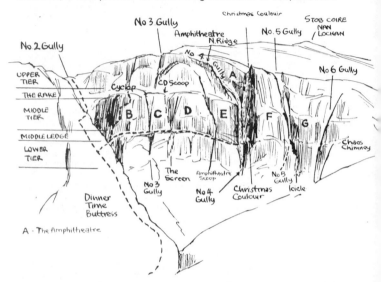

A - The Amphitheatre.

The entry to Middle Ledge from Dinner-time Buttress is made by crossing into the lowest part of the easy upper section of No. 2 Gully and following an awkward outward-sloping shelf (frequently iced) gently upwards and round the corner to the r. This is Grade II and highly spectacular. An easier approach to Middle Ledge is to cross No. 2 Gully low down and follow the lower ridge of B Buttress—mainly steep grass with short scrambling sections (Grade I). The Rake is easily gained from near the top of No. 2 Gully giving access to the climbs on the upper tier. It also provides an easy escape above the middle tier if time is pressing.

**Cyclop.** 350 ft. Grade III/IV. 2/4 hours. H. MacInnes and G.S.W.C. party. Jan. 1970. At the start of Middle Ledge a steep corner goes directly up B Buttress. Climb this to easier ground above. Take chimney line above this to gain an eye in the buttress. From other side of eye climb iced rock to the top.

**No. 3 Gully.** 1,000 ft. Grade II/III. 4 hrs. Crofton and Evans. March. 1934. This gully, immediately r. of B Buttress, is shallow and rather indefinite except where it cuts through the middle tier and numerous escapes are possible.

**The Screen.** 250 ft. Grade IV. 3-4 hrs. D. Bathgate and J. Brumfitt. Feb., 1965. The obvious large icefall which forms over the lowest tier of rocks to the r. of No. 3 Gully. It is the direct start to C-D Scoop which lies between C and D Buttresses on the middle tier. Up for 70 ft. to an icicle recess, traversing r. and then back l. above them to the final steep ice runnel.

**C. Buttress.** 500 ft. Grade II. 2 hrs. A. Taylor, A. Thompson, K. Withall. A. Smith and J. McArtney. 26th Feb., 1969. Entry to Middle Ledge may be made from Dinner-time Buttress or the lower part of B Buttress. Start up a short wide chimney on the r. and thereafter follow the well defined crest.

**C-D Scoop.** 500 ft. Grade II. 1 hr. from Middle Ledge to The Rake. D. Bathgate and J. Brumfitt. Feb., 1965. This, the continuation of the Screen, gives a relatively easy but interesting climb up the Middle tier. Entry should preferably be made from Dinner-time Buttress. It is the second gully on the l. (when traversing rightwards along Middle Ledge) which gives two short ice pitches to The Rake. A good finish, giving one further short pitch, is by the hidden r. branch of the gully to the l. (i.e. the continuation of No. 3 Gully above The Rake).

**D Buttress.** 500 ft. Grade II/III. 2 hrs. P. Mallinson, D. Power, J. Choat, J. Friend and l. Clough. 26th Feb., 1969. Starts from Middle Ledge by an obvious steep icy gang-way just to the r. of C-D Scoop. Above, zig-zagging ramps and ledges (r., l. and then r. again) lead to the crest where a short steep grooved wall is followed by easier climbing.

**Amphitheatre Scoop.** 800 ft. Grade IV. 4-6 hrs. I. Clough, G. Lowe and J. Hardie. 18th Feb., 1966. Starts from Middle Ledge between D and E Buttresses. The first 150 ft. follows a very steep column of ice in the back of a corner. After this the angle eases and the upper gully is followed to The Rake whence an easy continuation slants l. to the top.

**D Buttress Final Tier.** 300 ft. Grade II 1 hr. D. Power, P. Hardman, J. Friend, A. Thompson and A. Fyffe. 27th Feb., 1969. This climb, starting from The Rake, follows a shallow gully fault above the l. end of the D Buttress middle tier. It gives a short ice pitch near the foot and then easy snow leading to an awkward chockstone finish.

**Amphitheatre North Ridge.** 300 ft. Grade III/III. 1 hr. R. Viveash, K. Withall, A. Taylor, J. Choat and l. Clough. 27th Feb., 1969. This relatively easy but finely situated ridge gives a good finish above The Rake for the routes up the middle tier l. of No. 4 Gully. It starts above and slightly r. of the easy upper gully of Amphitheatre Scoop. A series of awkward little cracks and grooves lead up the front of the steep step to the crest.

**No. 4 Gully.** 1000 ft. Grade III/IV. 4-6 hrs. J. Brown·and D. Whillans. Dec., 1952. The obvious big deep gully near the centre of the face. It gives several ice pitches, those below the level of Middle Ledge being particularly difficult, or avoided by traversing into the gully via Middle Ledge. The gully continues immediately under the huge side wall of E Buttress until an easy ramp leads leftwards above it to join The Rake (a possible escape l. to the upper part of No. 2 gully). The gully however narrows to a deep cleft and continues, upwards to the l.h. side of the Amphitheatre and finally to the l.. to gain the summit slopes.

**Christmas Couloir.** 800 ft. Grade III/IV. 3-4 hrs. I. Clough and D. G. Roberts. 25th Dec., 1965. Starts from the level of Middle Ledge (which is the best approach) and follows an obvious rake cum couloir above and to the r. of the bed of No. 4 Gully and l. of F Buttress. There is a steep section to the r. of the buttress which appears to block the upper part of No. 4 Gully. This gives the crux and is often heavily iced. Above this the route continues up the r.h. side of the huge recess in the upper cliffs (The Amphitheatre ) above which there are three obvious finishes. the direct one being the most difficult.

**F Buttress Route.** 900 ft. Grade III/IV 2/5 hours. H. MacInnes, G.S.W.C. party. Jan. 1969. The start of this route is to the l. of the variant start to No. 5 Gully (described below). Take easiest line up to continuation of Middle Ledge. This lower section is seldom in winter condition. From the Middle Ledge continuation ascend upper section of buttress via the Needle's Eye, which is the deep rock chimney just to the l. of the upper part of No. 5 Gully.

**No. 5 Gully.** 1,000 ft. Grade III. 4-6 hrs. A. Fyffe, Catherine MacInnes and Niki Clough 18th Feb., 1969. A gigantic icicle forms on the overhanging wall which prevents direct access to this gully. The entry is made by an obvious short, shallow, slanting gully to the l., moving out and up on the r. where it steepens, to gain a ridge to the l. of the gully bed and below a deep chimney. A r. traverse leads into the gully where a steep ice pitch is climbed to the easier upper section. This gives one further 150 ft. ice pitch set at a relatively easy angle.

**No. 6 Gully.** 800 ft. Grade IV. 4-6 hrs. D. H. Munro and P. D. Smith. 30th March, 1951. The long gully on the r.h. side of the face which develops into an almost continuous cataract of ice. When it is in condition it gives one of the best climbs in Glencoe.

**Chaos Chimney.** 450 ft. Grade III. 3 hrs. A. Fyffe, E. Viveash, B. Jenkins, P. Hardman and J. Snodgrass. 26th Feb., 1969. The chimney-gully to the r. of No. 6 Gully which ends about half-way up the cliff. From the foot of No. 6 Gully, two short ice pitches lead up to an 80 ft. pitch in the narrows. Two further large pitches lead to the top.

---

# CLIMBS FROM COIRE NAM BEITH

The magnificent northern corrie of Bidean is contained in the horseshoe ridges linking Stob Coire nan Lochan, Bidean nam Bian, Bidean's West Top, Stob Coire nam Beith and the nose of An t-Sron. The main cliffs are the Diamond and Churchdoor Buttresses on the N. face of Bidean nam Bian, the westward facing cliff on the flank of the N. Spur of the W. Top and the immense cone of cliff leading to the summit of Stob nam Beith.

There are two approaches. One route starts immediately west of the main road bridge over the River Coe (opposite the Clachaig road end) and climbs steeply up the hillside by a well marked track which leads up into the corrie to cross the stream where it bifurcates. A subsidiary corrie leads up straight ahead to the col between Stob Coire nam Beith and An t-Sron. This gives the easiest route to the summit of Bidean (via the summits of Stob Coire nam Beith and the West Top) and is one of the best routes for descent. From the junction of the two streams the track leads up to the l. and up through a band of rock bluffs to the floor of the main corrie beneath the cliffs of Stob Coire nam Beith.

The other approach route also arrives in the corrie at this point. It starts as for the approach to the West Face of Aonach Dubh, gaining the foot of Dinner-time buttress and crossing No. 2 gully. It then uses the lower slopes of the West Face following, for much of the way, an old wire fence which leads up steeply and then by a gentle rising traverse into the floor of the corrie. The corrie continues up to a higher basin (often referred to as the Bidean Corrie), beneath the Churchdoor and Diamond Buttresses. Leading up steeply on either side of these two big buttresses are easy slopes to the cols between Stob Coire nan Lochan and Bidean and between Bidean and the West Top. Both of these give descent routes but care should be exercised as they can become very icy. To the r. (west) of this upper basin is another subsidiary corrie which leads up, between the cliffs of the West Top spur and Stob Coire nam Beith, to a shallow col between the two summits. This gives another, recommendable, descent route although one should not glissade as there are a number of small rock outcrops in the corrie which may be hidden from above.

# BIDEAN NAM BIAN (3,766 ft.)

### DIAMOND BUTTRESS:

**North Route.** 700 ft. Grade II/III. 2-4 hrs. J. Clarkson and F. King. 6th Feb., 1955. Skirts round the l.h. edge of the buttress following a series of chimneys and scoops which lead to a final rocky arête. Often easy to escape to the l. so that the route lacks seriousness. A slightly more difficult start (Grade III. L. S. Lovat and W. Harrison, 13th March, 1955) is to follow an obvious steep scoop, near but to the r. of the normal route, which leads to an arête on the r. The arête is followed by a short traverse into another scoop and then the line goes up and l. to regain the normal route about 250 ft. up.

**Direct Route.** 500 ft. Grade IV. 4-5 hrs. M. Noon and J. McLean. Jan., 1959. Finds a way up the central wall of the buttress to gain the r.h. end of a long ledge which cuts horizontally across to the l. edge of the buttress at about half height. The line continues by grooves upwards and to the r. to emerge on the r.h. ridge shortly before the summit of the buttress.

**Central Gully.** 700 ft. Grade I or II (depending on variations followed). A fine route to the summit of Bidean. Start to the r. of Collie's Pinnacle and continue directly to the top, normally a straight-forward snow climb. By starting to the l. of the Pinnacle and taking the r. fork (about 250 ft. above the neck of the Pinnacle) one should obtain a good route of grade II standard with two short pitches, leading to the top of Churchdoor Buttress. There are also several variation exits to the l. above the neck of the Pinnacle.

## CHURCHDOOR BUTTRESS:

**West Chimney Route.** 700 ft. Grade IV. 4-5 hrs. A. Fyffe and H. MacInnes. 8th Feb., 1969. Up to the r. of the lowest rocks of the buttress is a snow bay leading to an obvious deep chimney, which is followed past two difficult chockstones to a cave where there is a through-route. Beyond another chimney a ledge system leads l. to the top of the Arch, an airy platform formed by two huge jammed boulders. Above a hard 30 ft. corner chimney the route continues up to the l. to the summit.

**The Gangway.** 200 ft. Grade II. ½ hr. A. Fyffe and H. MacInnes. 8th Feb., 1969. An obvious line high up on the r.h. wall of the buttress, slanting up to the l. to reach the top.

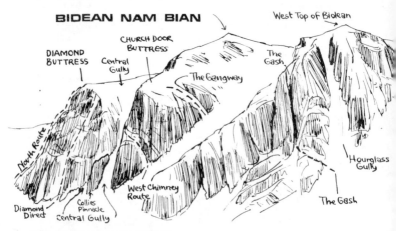

## THE WEST TOP OF BIDEAN

These cliffs are on the western flank of the spur which descends northwards into Coire nam Beith from the West Top (i.e. The highest point on the ridge between the summits of Bidean and Stob Coire nam Beith).

**Hourglass Gully.** 400 ft. Grade 1. High up on the cliffs towards the summit ridge is this long tapering gully which opens out to a snow fan below the top. Steep and generally straight-forward but sometimes giving one or two short easy steps.

**The Gash.** 400 ft. Grade III/IV. 2 hrs. I. Clough, M. Hadley and M. Large. 22nd March, 1959. The steep upper cliffs to the l. of Hourglass Gully are split by a narrow, deep-cleft gully, gained by a rising left-ward traverse from the foot of Hourglass Gully or it may be reached directly. A ledge on the r. gives the best stance before a long run-out up the steep runnel at the deep section which usually gives a series of short bulging ice pitches. Above the long runnel the way is barred by a 15ft. overhanging chockstone which is best climbed on the l. to a cave below a second huge chockstone slab. An intriguing through-route leads up snow in the back of the cave to a very tight exit.

## STOB COIRE NAM BEITH (3,621 ft.)

The base of this massive and complicated cone of cliffs swings through a great arc so that all the climbs cannot be seen from any one viewpoint. The r.h. section is clearly seen from the junction of the streams on the first approach route. The most obvious feature here is the long Summit Gully. The slabby 300 ft. Pyramid and (above and l. of it) the bigger and steeper Sphinx buttress form an indefinite ridge which bounds Summit Gully on the l. To the l. of these is the region

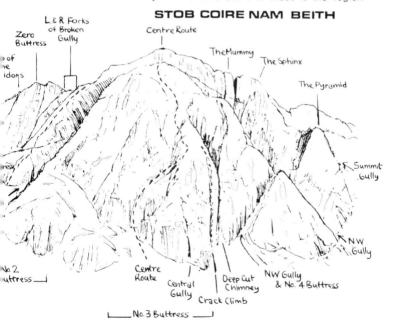

STOB COIRE NAM BEITH

where the vague North-west Gully winds its way through the broken rocks of No. 4 Buttress. The topography of the important central section can be seen in the diagram—the unmistakable Deep-cut Chimney, the rightward-slanting ramp-gully start of No. 4 Buttress, the chimney-groove line of Crack Climb, the long shallow ice-course of Central Gully. Beyond Central Gully the cliffs on the l.h. side of the cone fall back and eventually form a very big bay. Arch Gully runs up the r.h. side of the bay and to the l. of the lower part of this is a big rock 'rognon' split by a narrow chimney line, the start of the so-called No. 1 Buttress. Above this rognon is a broad sloping snowshelf and the continuation of the No. 1 Buttress chimney-line which leads up the rocks at the back of the bay. A shallow gully curls up and round the l.h. side of the rognon to the snow shelf. This is the approach to Broken Gully which has two forks, and lies in the l.h. recess of the bay. It leads up to the l. to emerge on a shoulder. Beyond Broken Gully the final bold projection below the shoulder is called Zero Buttress.

**The Corridors.** 500 ft. Grade III/IV. 3 hrs. I. Clough, Mary Anne Hudson, C. Hutchinson, Cynthia Williamson and D. Davies. 12th Feb., 1969. The face of Zero Buttress is cut by two shallow square-cut gully sections; the first ending at a ledge about 150 ft. up and the other starting from this ledge a little further to the r. and leading through to the top of the buttress. This gives the line of the climb which is steep and sustained for the first 300 ft. The second corridor should give two ice pitches, a short one at the entry and a 30 ft. runnel tapering to a bulge below the final easy angled section. From the shoulder at the top of the buttress one can continue easily to the summit or walk into the subsidiary corrie on the l.

**Broken Gully.** 500 ft. Grade II. 1½ hrs. Mr. and Mrs. I. Clough. 13th Jan., 1966. The gully goes l. up into the recess above the broad snow shelf which splits No. 1 Buttress into two tiers. After about 100 ft. a shallow gully on the r. is followed until an easy leftwards traverse leads out to the top of Zero Buttress. The l. fork (I. Clough and party. 25th Jan., 1967) is the direct continuation and is separated from the normal route by a rock rib. It is steeper and holds more ice (grade II/III).

**No. 1 Buttress.** 700 ft. Grade II/III. 2 hrs. I. Clough and party. 9th March, 1967. The chimney line up the rognon and the upper tier above the broad snow shelf gives a series of short ice pitches. Above the chimneys it is possible to continue to the summit or traverse easily to the l. to reach the shoulder at the top of Zero Buttress.

**Arch Gully.** 800 ft. Grade II/III. 1½-3 hrs. C. M. Allan and J. H. B. Bell. Dec., 1933. To the r. of No. 1 Buttress. The first section can give one or two short easy pitches but is generally banked up. A straightforward tapering and steepening slope leads to two steep ice pitches which should be climbed directly to the top, but can be turned without much difficulty. Easy slopes lead to the summit, 400 ft. above.

**Centre Route.** 1500 ft. Grade II/III. 3-5 hrs. J. G. Parish, D. H. Haworth and D. B. McIntyre. Feb., 1945. This is the longest buttress on the mountain and gives an excellent winter climb, serious on account of its length. The route starts round to the l. of the lowest rocks of No. 3

Buttress (i.e. l. of Central Gully) and zig-zags up the flank of the buttress for the first steep 200 ft. The angle decreases higher up.

**Central Gully.** 1,500 ft. Grade III/IV. 3-5 hrs. J. Clarkson and J. Waddell. 12th Jan., 1958. The shallow gully which starts above and slightly l. of the lowest rocks of No. 3 Buttress is a natural ice trap and when in condition gives one of the best routes in the corrie.

**Crack Climb.** 1,500 ft. Grade II/III. 3 hrs. L. S. Lovat and N. G. Harthill. 12th Jan., 1958. Follows the obvious chimney-groove on the projecting side wall to the l. of Deep-cut Chimney, starting about 80 ft. up. The line leads to the foot of a steep 30 ft. wall which may be very hard. However an escape to the r. is possible, crossing into the amphitheatre of Deep-cut Chimney.

**Deep-cut Chimney.** 1,500 ft. Grade III/IV. 4-5 hrs. W. M. Mackenzie and W. H. Murray. April, 1939. The chimney which is really a deep narrow gully, should give 3 or 4 steep ice pitches generally short, though one may be more than 40 ft. high. After 400 ft. the gully comes out into a small amphitheatre from which it is possible to escape to easier ground by going up to the r. to the crest of No. 4 Buttress near the fork of the N.W. Gully. However, the Left Fork from the amphitheatre gives further difficulties and can be particularly hard if plated in verglass. It goes up to the l. following a long steep crack-line which eventually joins the common finish for the No. 3 Buttress routes.

**No. 4 Buttress.** 1,500 ft. Grade II. 2-3 hrs. Start up the rightward slanting ramp/gully to the r. of the Deep-cut chimney. This leads up and round the corner into N.W. Gully. From the gully it is possible to move back l. to the crest of the ridge almost anywhere and follow it leftwards up the face.

**North-west Gully.** 1,500 ft. Grade II. 2-3 hrs. Glover and Worsdell. April, 1906. In common with the previous climb, this route is open to considerable variation. Probably the best approach is to use the slanting gully of No. 4 Buttress but it is possible to traverse in from the r., from the base of the Pyramid. Straight-forward snow leads up to the l. of the Sphinx Buttress, beyond which the gully has two forks. The l. fork continues directly without much interest. The r. fork leads up to the l. of the upper part of the Sphinx for several hundred feet until it forks again below The Mummy. The rock scenery on this section is impressive. The l. fork is the best and sometimes gives a short pitch leading up to a shoulder. A steep wall to the l. of the shoulder gives the crux of the climb and can be quite hard when iced. Above this several hundred feet of easier climbing lead to the summit.

**Summit Gully.** 1,500 ft. Grade I/II. 2 hrs. The great long gully which starts just to the l. of the lowest r.h. rocks of the Stob Coire nam Beith cone of cliffs. It is generally straight-forward. Some route-finding ability is necessary but despite occasional forks it is not difficult to keep to the main line. It is generally best to turn difficulties on the r. The gully emerges only a few yards from the summit cairn.

**AN T-SRON (2,750 ft.).** The following two climbs are on the east face of An t-Sron (i.e. the r. wall of the subsidiary corrie between Stob Coire nam Beith and An t-Sron). There are several easy gullies further r. towards the nose of An t-Sron, but high in the corrie to the l. of these is a big mass of crags. The r.h. section includes a big prominent smooth slab. To the l. of this is a snow bay at a slightly higher level from which rise steep twin diverging couloirs. These two obvious lines give the climbs.

**Sac-o-Coal Couloir.** 500 ft. Grade III. 1½ hrs. J. McArtney, D. Selby, B. Payne, J. Lines and G. Drayton. 18th Feb., 1969. The l.h. line leads to a very steep and awkward corner exit before a final easy slope leads to the summit ridge.

**Smashed Spectacles Gully.** 500 ft. Grade II/III. 1½ hrs. I. Clough, F. Jones, R. Fox and C. Wood. 18th Feb., 1969. The r.h. line gives a short ice pitch in the first section and then follows a very steep chimney capped by an ice bulge before an easier continuation leads to the top.

**The Chasm of An t-Sron.** 1,200 ft. Grade II/III. 4 hrs. H. M. Brown, J. Matyssek, R. K. Graham and M. Smith. 2nd Jan., 1963. The great gully which splits the north face. The first pitch is normally turned but the other pitches higher up give good sport in icy conditions.

---

# CLIMBS ON THE AONACH EAGACH

The Aonach Eagach is the long ridge which bounds Glencoe on the north, the name (the 'notched ridge') applying particularly to the narrow crest extending between Sgor nam Fionnaidh on the west to Am Bodach at the east end. The Glencoe flank of this ridge is steep and complex, very rocky and seamed by many gullies.

**The Aonach Eagach Traverse.** About 2 miles, top to top. Grade I/II. 3-6 hrs. In good weather and conditions the winter traverse of this ridge gives a very fine expedition. The normal route is from E. to W. which gives one the advantage of 400 ft. less to climb. Best starting point is from near the white cottage of Allt-na-reigh. (Parking space at the signpost to the Meeting of Three Waters bridge, on the r. going up the glen). Starting just below the cottage a track leads up, crossing the stream, into the corrie to the east of Am Bodach whence easy slopes lead leftwards to the top (3,085 ft.). Alternatively one may continue directly up the ridge to the summit from the start (harder—in descent this route is best avoided). The descent to the west from Am Bodach can be quite difficult, go slightly r. for a few feet then back l., and down a gully-crack.

The most interesting section of the ridge is between Meall Dearg (3,118 ft.) and Stob Coire Leith (3,080 ft.), particularly a very narrow pinnacled section and an awkward slabby descent beyond it.

**The difficulty and the time taken can vary enormously with conditions; in exceptionally hard conditions the climb could give a very long day with difficulties approaching Grade III standard.** The safest descent is to continue from Sgor nam Fionnaidh to reach the saddle before the Pap of Glencoe before cutting diagonally back across the slope to the

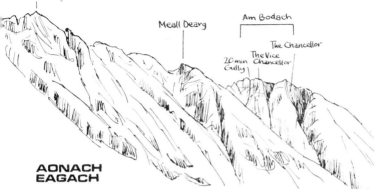

Stob Coire Leith
Meall Dearg
Am Bodach
The Chancellor
The Vice Chancellor
20 min Gully

## AONACH EAGACH

I. to meet the old road in the vicinity of the Youth Hostel. The shallow corrie leading down from Sgor nam Fionnaidh towards Loch Achtriochtan is also straight-forward but steep and due regard should be paid to snow conditions as there was once an avalanche fatality here. Another descent route goes directly down to the Clachaig Inn but it is not easy to follow and care should be taken to avoid the numerous crags on this slope and especially the deep gash of Clachaig Gully. **There are no safe descents on the Glencoe side of the ridge between the two end peaks.** It is far better to continue to the end of the ridge before attempting to descend or, if really pressed, to descend to the north.

The chief merit of the following climbs is that they receive sunshine and because of this may often be in good condition before other climbing areas. They are useful early in the season and the buttresses are good even with only a powder snow covering. Competent parties could possibly take in one of these routes as a start to the traverse of the ridge. The easiest descent is to go down the corrie to the west of Am Bodach.

**The Chancellor.** 1,000 ft. Grade II/III. 3 hrs. W. Skidmore and R. Richardson. Dec., 1965. The Chancellor is a big prominent buttress falling to the south-west from the summit of Am Bodach and bounded on either side by deep gullies, that on the r. being particularly conspicuous. Best viewed from the main road about half a mile east of Achtriochtan farmhouse and the direct approach from this point is relatively simple. The main difficulty of the route is route-finding, particularly on the steep middle section where the best way lies to the l.

**The Vice Chancellor.** 700 ft. Grade II/III. 2 hrs. H. MacInnes and G.S.W.C. party. 18th Feb., 1969. The next buttress to the l. of The Chancellor. Route-finding again gives much of the interest and there are some fine situations.

**Twenty Minute Gully.** 600 ft. Grade I/II. 20 minutes! H. MacInnes and

G.S.W.C. party. Jan., 1969. A pleasant little gully to the l. of the Vice Chancellor. There is an indefinite scoop between the two.

**Red Funnel Gully.** 600 ft. Grade II/III. 1½ hrs. R. Baillie, H. MacInnes and G.S.W.C. parties. Circa 1964. An excellent training climb for a short day in hard icy conditions. It is on the S.E. face of A' Chailleach (the peak to the east of Am Bodach) and starts only 20 minutes from the road. The best parking layby is on the l. shortly after the main road enters the gorge and before the sharp bend to the l. Walk up onto the old road and follow it rightwards for a short distance. Red Funnel Gully is the l.-most of several on the face and has an indefinite gully starting just to its r. A series of short ice pitches following the stream-bed lead to a deeper section. Here, a steep 40 ft. ice pitch (crux) is followed by a passage beneath a huge chockstone and a final steep icy chimney-groove. The quickest descent is by a long descending traverse to the E. but one may continue easily to the top of the mountain and descend by the corrie between A' Chailleach and Am Bodach.

---

# OUTLYING CLIMBS FROM GLENCOE

## STOB A' GHLAIS CHOIRE (3,207 ft.)—SRON NA CREISE.

The N.E. face of 'Sron na Creise' is seamed by several gullies which appear to be incredibly steep. However the face will normally give only Grade I climbing in the gullies, possibly attaining Grade II on the ridges and buttresses. The easiest descent is down the northern spur (some rock steps; best avoided on the l. in descent) but the face climb should preferably be followed by continuing south to Clachlet or Meall a' Bhuiridh.

**SRON NA LAIRIG.** 1,000 ft. Grade I/II. 2-3 hrs. J. Black, C. Montgomery, Miss A. Williamson and Miss R. McCulloch. Nov., 1949. A prominent rocky spur overlooking the head of the Lairig Eilde and leading up on-to the S.E. ridge of Stob Coire Sgreamhach. The approach up the Lairig is quite long (about 2½ miles) but gentle. The lower part of the ridge is broad and much variation is possible but higher up it is well defined and narrows to a very airy arête. It gives a pleasant climb, comparable with but much less strenuous than, the Aonach Eagach.

**SGOR NA H-ULAIDH** (3,258 ft.). This fine but rather remote peak lies to the S.W. of Bidean. The approach takes about 2 hours. Follow a side road southwards from a junction with the main road about a mile west of the Clachaig road-end. This leads to the farmhouse of Ghleann-leac-na-muidhe and from there the glen continues south and then slightly east to end in Coire Dubh beneath the north face of the mountain.

**Red Gully.** 650 ft. Grade III. 3-4 hrs. D. Scott, J. C. Henderson and R. Anderson. Feb., 1950. The conspicuous deep gully immediately below the summit. It should give three or four good ice pitches. The third is usually the crux but it can be turned on the r.

**Subsidiary Scoop.** 500 ft. Grade II. 1½ hrs. **Mr.** and **Mrs. I.** Clough. 31st March, 1966. This is a shallow gully immediately l. of Red Gully and separated from it by a rocky rib. It usually gives one or two short steps of ice.

**Vixen Gully.** 800 ft. Grade I. 1 hr. R. Anderson, J. G. Black and G. Allison (in descent). March, 1948. The broad long gully in the middle of the face to the r. of Red Gully gives a straight-forward snow climb.

**Humpback Gully.** 1,000 ft. Grade II. 2 hrs. J. Renny, I. MacEacheran, R. Sharp and W. Sproul. Nov., 1965. This climb is also from Coire Dubh but is on the r.h. side; on the north-east face of Creag Bhan. It is the obvious gully to the r. of the summit.

## INDEX: BEN NEVIS AREA

n.c.—exceptionally hard climbs not given a star rating.

## INDEX: GLENCOE AREA

64

# NEW CLIMBS

# cicerone press
# Publications

CAVES, POTHOLES & MINES OF DERBYSHIRE
*J. Ballard* **£1.00**

WINTER CLIMBS, NEVIS & GLENCOE
*Clough & MacInnes* **90p**

WINTER CLIMBS, CAIRNGORMS,
MEAGHAIDH, LOCHNAGAR *Cunningham* **90p**

WINTER CLIMBS, NORTH WALES *Newcombe* **£1.00**

MODERN SNOW & ICE TECHNIQUES *March* **£1.00**

MODERN ROPE TECHNIQUES IN MOUNTAINEERING
*March* **£1.50**

RHUM *Hamish Brown* **£1.00**

ROCK CLIMBS, ISLE OF MAN *Gartrell* **50p**

ROCK CLIMBS, LANCASHIRE & THE NORTH WEST
*Ainsworth* **£2.00**

WALKS & CLIMBS IN ROMSDAL, NORWAY *Howard*

HILLWALKING IN SNOWDONIA *Rowland* **£1.00**

THE ASCENT OF SNOWDON *Rowland* **40p**

THE TOUR OF MONT BLANC *Harper* **£1.50**

HELSBY & THE WIRRAL *Rouse* **£1.50**

SONAMARG (Kashmir) *Jackson* **£1.80**

WALKS ON THE WEST PENNINE MOORS    *Sellers*   **£1.50**
LLANYMYNECH QUARRY          *Caine & Bennett*   **75p**
MOUNTAIN BIBLIOGRAPHY              *W. Neate*
WALKS & CLIMBS IN THE PYRENEES    *K. Reynolds*   **£1·80**
LLANBERIS AREA (TOURIST GUIDE)        *S. Styles*

From all good climbing shops. In case of difficulty from
Cicerone Press, Harmony Hall, Milnthorpe, Cumbria LA7 7QE
(Add 10p per book p+p)

CLIMBER & rambler

OFFICIAL MAGAZINE OF THE B.M.C.

the monthly magazine for winter and summer